So!

YOU WANT TO BECOME
A GRAPHIC DESIGNER

A RESOURCE AND GUIDE

Carole Maugé-Lewis, MFA

Professor Emerita of Kennesaw State University

© 2024 by Carole Maugé-Lewis. All rights reserved.

This book is protected by copyright law. No part of this publication may be reproduced,
distributed, or transmitted in any form or by any means, including photocopying, recording, or other
electronic or mechanical methods, without the prior written permission of the copyright owner,
except in the case of brief quotations embodied in critical reviews and certain other
noncommercial uses permitted by copyright law.

The author has taken great care to ensure that all the information in this publication is accurate.
However, the author cannot be held responsible for any loss, damage, or disruptions caused by errors or omissions.
The majority of the design work in this book were created by students who studied graphic design under the author's
guidance, and permission to use them has been obtained. Any other images are protected by a standard license
purchased from Vecteezy. AI technology was used to help with minor content editing in this book.

Cover design by the author.

ISBN: 979-8-9904141-0-5

For corrections, inquiries about interviews or speaking engagements, please contact
mymaugedesign@gmail.com

DEDICATION

This book is dedicated to aspiring graphic design students, career changers, self-taught designers, entry-level designers, Art and Design students, creative entrepreneurs, design enthusiasts, and especially to educators and instructors, who want additional resources to guide their students in graphic design studies.

ACKNOWLEDGMENTS

I express my gratitude to The Almighty for guidance and blessings received throughout the process of creating this book, my initial publication in my field of expertise.

Thank you to everyone who has played a role in bringing this book to fruition. Your contributions have made a significant impact, and I am truly appreciative.

Foreword:
Gordon Kaye: I am profoundly grateful to you for graciously penning the foreword for my debut book. Your insightful words and endorsement are invaluable additions to this project. Thank you for sharing your wisdom and support, and for being an integral part of this journey.

Book Cover:
Valerie Dibble: In heartfelt appreciation for your invaluable insights and feedback on the book cover design, contributing to its refinement and its overall visual impact.

Testimonials:
Dr. Sandra Bird: To my colleague and former interim Chair of the School of Art and Design. Your endorsement holds significant meaning for me. Thank you for believing in my work and for your invaluable contribution and genuine support of this endeavor.

Ayokunle Odeleye: A special thanks to my esteemed colleague whose testimonial adds depth and credibility to this book. Your genuine support and endorsement are truly appreciated.

Linda McCulloch: A genuine thank you for your kind words and endorsement. Your fervent support has added credibility and encouragement to this project.

Michael Gaston: Colleague, friend and companion during our years with a for-profit college. Your seal of approval means a great deal to me, and I am thankful.

Editors:
Cherie K. Miller has an MA in Professional Writing and an MA Certificate in American Studies from Kennesaw State University. She was an educational professional for almost 20 years, serving in the Coles College of Business and the Radow College of Humanities. She has written or co-written four books and has over 200 published articles in magazines. Cherie is passionate about reading and the written word. She was thrilled to contribute to this series!

Linda McCulloch: Graduate of the Ringling School of Art and Design, Owner of *Design That Works*, an award-winning graphic design and marketing communications company (since 1987). Linda graciously shared her knowledge and expertise during our class critiques and offered to review, proofread and edit the manuscript.

I extend my sincere gratitude to the students who generously granted permission for their award-winning designs to be featured in this book. Your creativity and willingness to share your work have greatly enriched its content.

For the unwavering support of my son Kevin, who has always stood by me and been enthusiastic about my journey as an author, many thanks.

Carole

FOREWORD

In the realm of creative pursuits, graphic design stands at the vibrant intersection of artistry and functionality. Aspiring designers embark on a journey of visual storytelling, weaving narratives through the seamless integration of color, typography, and form. In this digital era, the allure of graphic design has grown exponentially, attracting self-taught enthusiasts, career changers, and those who thirst for the fusion of creativity and technology.

This book, authored by an expert in the field of design education and a superb practitioner in her own right, Professor Carole Maugé-Lewis, emerges as a guiding beacon for those entering the dynamic world of graphic design. As a distinguished professor emerita, she not only nurtured creativity within the fertile grounds of academia but also witnessed the flourishing of countless design careers under her guidance.

Professor Maugé-Lewis has been the driving force behind the development of a well-recognized graphic design program at Kennesaw State University, a Georgia institution synonymous with excellence in design education. Her illustrious career has been marked by many accolades, including the prestigious Distinguished Teaching Award bestowed upon her not once, but twice. These honors attest to her unwavering commitment to nurturing the next generation of designers and design visionaries.

Over decades as publisher of Graphic Design USA (GDUSA) magazine and website, I have had the pleasure of watching Professor Maugé-Lewis work her magic. Recognized as an "Educator to Watch" and a "Person to Watch" by the editors of GDUSA, she has carved a niche as a trailblazer in the design landscape. Her influence extends beyond the classroom, permeating the industry through the achievements of her students. These budding designers, under her guidance, have been the recipients of numerous graphic design awards and, more importantly, transitioned seamlessly into thriving professional roles.

This book is a testament to Professor Maugé-Lewis's dedication to making design education accessible to all. It caters not only to eager beginners, navigating the labyrinth of design principles, but also to seasoned educators and instructors seeking insights to enhance their teaching approaches. It is a comprehensive resource, a compendium of wisdom distilled from years of experience, enriched with her students' works, practical advice and industry insights.

As you delve into the following pages, let this book be your companion on the exciting journey of becoming a graphic designer. May Professor Maugé-Lewis's legacy of excellence in graphic design education inspire and guide you as you unfold the canvas of your own creative path.

Gordon Kaye
Publisher
Graphic Design USA/GDUSA/GDUSA.COM

QUOTE BY SAUL BASS

"Design is thinking
made visual"

TABLE OF
CONTENTS

TABLE OF CONTENTS

INTRODUCTION

At its core, graphic design merges form and function, bringing together artistic expression with effective communication. Whether you're designing a logo that captures a brand's identity, crafting captivating layouts for websites and print materials, or conceptualizing visually striking marketing campaigns, graphic designers play a crucial role in shaping the visual landscape of our world.

To succeed in this dynamic field, aspiring graphic designers need a diverse skill set. Proficiency in design software like the Adobe Creative Suite is vital, but it's only the beginning.

Creativity is the lifeblood of graphic design, and having a keen eye for aesthetics is a must. In addition to technical skills, understanding the elements and the principles of design, typography, color theory, layout and composition are essential for creating impactful visual content.

Alongside technical and creative skills, effective communication and collaboration are key attributes for a graphic designer. Clients, colleagues, and stakeholders will rely on you to translate ideas into visual language, so being able to listen, interpret, and visualize concepts are crucial.

Are you ready to embark on a journey where creativity and strategy converge, and visual storytelling becomes your language of choice? Becoming a graphic designer is not just about acquiring skills; it's about cultivating a mindset that embraces continuous learning and adaptation to the ever-evolving design landscape.

So! if you really want to do graphic design for a living, you must LOVE it. Creating great design work should be a positive, JOYFUL feeling, as it still is for me and for several of my professional design colleagues. We agree that yes, it's hard work, but if you like it and become good at it, it won't really seem like work. And the best feeling of all is when you know your work is good, the client loves it, it meets all the standards set for the project, you get paid fairly, and and everyone is happy.

Let's explore the exciting world of graphic design and discover the boundless possibilities that await you. Peruse this comprehensive resource and guide covering topics such as fundamental design principles, software tools, the design process, the design critique, portfolio development, industry insights, and practical tips for career growth.

THE FUNDAMENTALS

Learning the fundamentals of graphic design is essential for aspiring designers as it lays the groundwork for their creative journey. Understanding concepts such as typography, color theory, composition, balance, white space and visual hierarchy among others, provides designers with the tools they need to effectively communicate their ideas visually. Mastering these fundamentals not only enhances design skills but also fosters a strong foundation upon which designers can build their unique style and approach. By honing their understanding of the basics, designers gain the confidence and competence needed to tackle more complex design challenges and produce impactful and visually compelling work.

Here are the key fundamentals to keep in mind:

1. Hierarchy: Establish a clear visual hierarchy to guide the viewer's attention through the design. Important elements should stand out, making the message or information easy to understand.

2. Balance: Achieve balance in your design by distributing elements and creating visual stability. Balance can be symmetrical (even distribution) or asymmetrical (uneven distribution, yet visually balanced), depending on your design goals.

3. Contrast: Use contrast to emphasize differences in elements like color, size, or shape. This creates visual interest and highlights important information, preventing monotony, and drawing attention to key elements.

4. Repetition: Consistently use visual elements such as colors, fonts, and shapes to establish unity and reinforce the overall design theme. Repetition creates cohesion and reinforces the brand or message.

5. Alignment: Proper alignment ensures that elements are logically positioned, creating a clean and organized appearance. Aligning elements establishes a sense of order and clarity in the design.

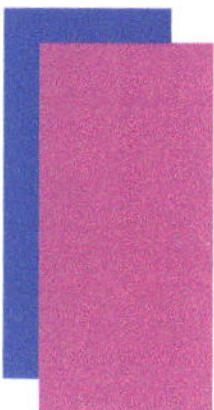

6. Proximity: Group related elements together to create a visual connection and organize information. Proximity can be used to signify relationships, making it easier for the viewer to understand the content.

7. Typography: Choose appropriate typefaces/fonts, sizes, and spacing for effective communication. Typography contributes to the overall aesthetic legibility and readability of the design.

8. Color Theory: Study and understand the psychology of color and its impact on emotions and perceptions. A well-chosen color palette enhances visual appeal and reinforces the intended message.

9. White Space (Negative Space): Effective use of white space prevents visual clutter and allows the viewer's eyes to rest. White space enhances readability and highlights key elements.

10. Grids and Layouts: Grid systems provide a framework for organizing content, ensuring consistency, and alignment. Well-structured layouts contribute to a professional, and visually pleasing design.

These fundamental principles serve as a guide for graphic designers to create compelling and purposeful visuals. Whether it's for print, digital media, branding, or any other form of visual communication, mastering these principles will enable designers to effectively communicate messages and create designs that resonate with their audience.

LEARN
THE PROGRAMS

To become a skilled graphic designer, it's essential to familiarize yourself with various design software tools and become proficient in some, especially those that are used in graphic design. The specific programs you should learn will depend on the type of design work you're interested in and the industry standards. Join a learning commmunity or take the inititative and create a learning group.

Here are some key graphic design software programs to consider:

Adobe Creative Cloud:
• Adobe Photoshop: Used for photo editing, image manipulation, and digital painting.
• Adobe Illustrator: Ideal for creating vector graphics, logos, and illustrations.
• Adobe InDesign: Primarily used for layout design, such as brochures, magazines, and books.

Sketch: A popular vector-based design tool for UX/UI (User Experience/User Interface) designers, used to create user interfaces and web designs.

Figma: A widely-used cloud-based design tool for collaborative design, particularly in web and app development.

CorelDRAW: Similar to Adobe Illustrator, CorelDRAW is a vector graphics editor that offers tools for illustration and page layout.

***Affinity Designer:** A cost-effective alternative to Adobe Illustrator, Affinity Designer is a vector graphic design software known for its speed and performance.

***Canva:** Although not as feature-rich as professional design tools, Canva is user-friendly and great for quick design projects, making it suitable for beginners.

Procreate: A powerful tool for digital illustration, Procreate is particularly useful for creating artwork on tablets.

Blender: If you're interested in 3D design and animation, Blender is an open-source software that allows you to create 3D models, animations, and visual effects.

Remember to stay updated with the latest versions of these programs, as technology and tools evolve. It's also beneficial to keep an eye on industry trends and be open to learning new tools as they emerge. Online tutorials, courses, and communities can be valuable resources to enhance your skills in using these graphic design programs.

***Canva has acquired the Affinity creative software suite. Visit their website for more details.**

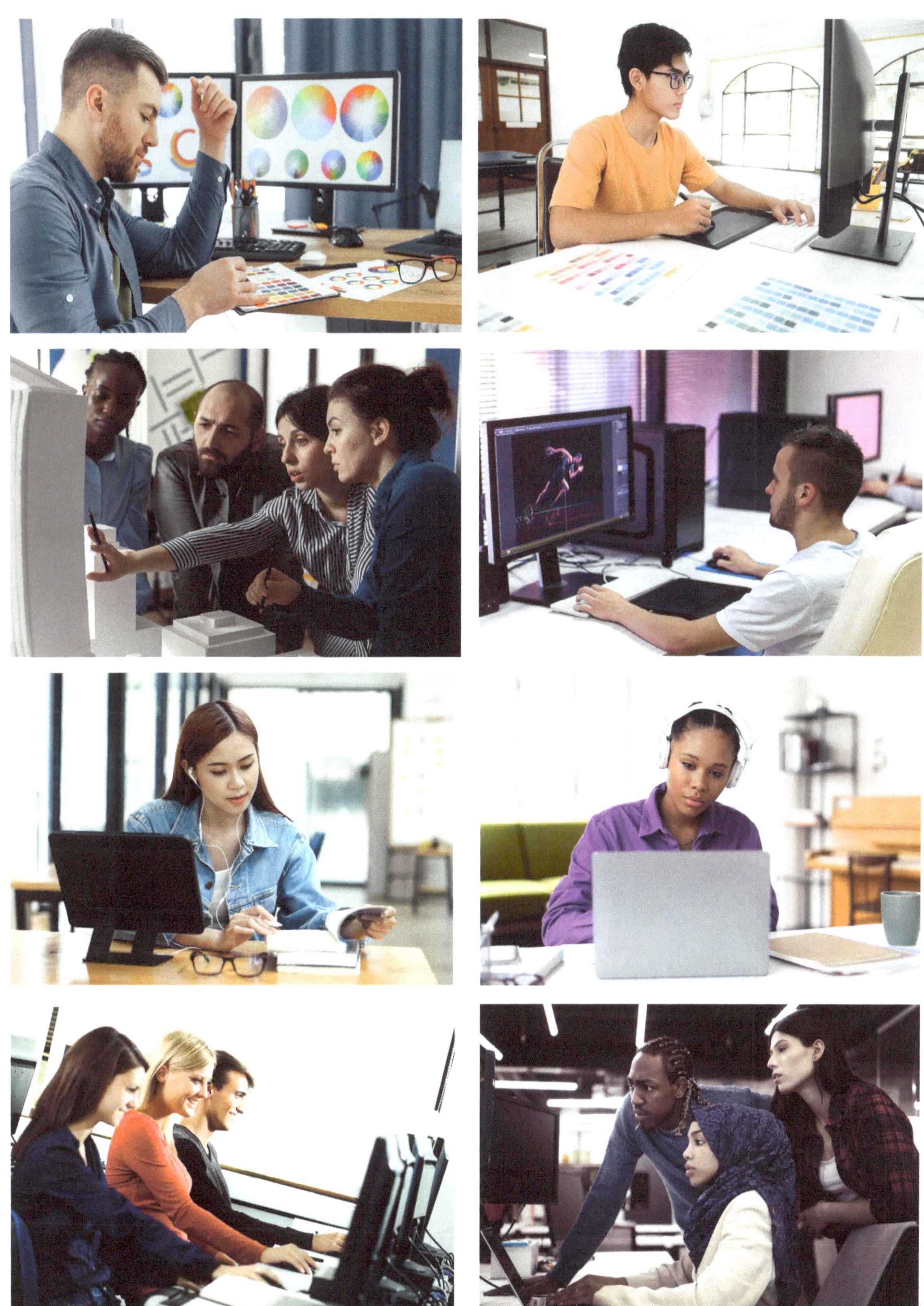

Learning new computer programs can be enjoyable, but trying to learn alone is not recommended. Learning in groups can be even more beneficial. Look for a learning community or a place where you can learn together with others. You can also learn together virtually.

THE VALUE OF JOINING DESIGN COMMUNITIES

Joining design communities can greatly benefit your growth as a graphic designer. These communities offer learning opportunities, networking potential, and the chance to share experiences with like-minded individuals.

Here are some reasons why you should consider joining design communities and where to find them:

Learning Opportunities:
Design communities often host webinars, workshops, and tutorials, where experienced designers share their knowledge and skills. Peer feedback can also help you improve your work and gain valuable insights into industry best practices.

Networking:
Connecting with other designers, whether beginners or seasoned professionals, can open doors to collaboration, job opportunities, and mentorship. Networking within design communities can expose you to different perspectives and approaches in the field.

Inspiration:
Design communities serve as hubs for creative inspiration. By viewing others' works and participating in discussions, you can ignite your creativity and familiarize yourself with new design trends.

Support and Encouragement:
Design can be a challenging field, but being part of a community provides a support system where you can seek advice, share struggles, and celebrate achievements.

Industry Updates:
Design communities often share news, updates, and discussions about the latest trends, tools, and technologies in the design industry.

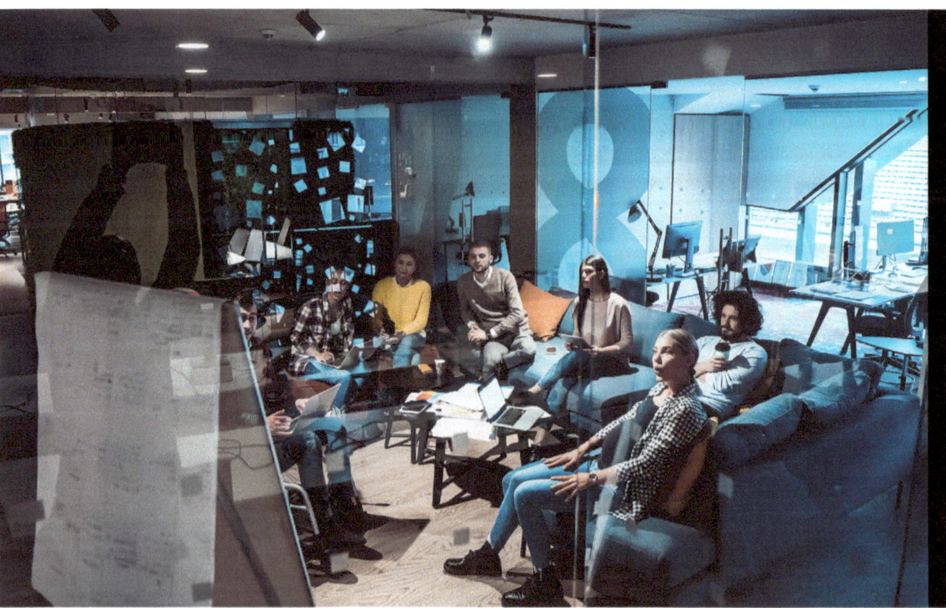

A design community of learners.

Places where you can find design communities

Online Platforms:

Behance: A platform by Adobe where designers showcase their portfolios and connect with others.

Dribbble: An online community for showcasing and discovering creative work, particularly in the fields of design and illustration.

DeviantArt: A community for artists and designers to showcase their work, receive feedback, and connect with others.

Forums:

Reddit (r/graphic_design): A subreddit for designers to share their work, seek advice, and engage in discussions.

Designer Hangout: An invite-only Slack community for designers to connect, collaborate, and share insights.

Social Media:

LinkedIn: Join design-related groups and follow relevant hashtags to connect with professionals in the field.

X (formerly known as Twitter): Follow designers, design agencies, and participate in design-related chats.

Local Meetups:

Check for local design meetups or events through platforms like Meetup.com. Meeting designers in person can lead to strong connections.

Remember to actively participate in discussions, share your work, and be open to feedback. Being part of design communities not only enhances your skills but also contributes to a sense of camaraderie within the design industry. Finding inspiration to create mockups is vital for developing unique and captivating design ideas.

THE IMPORTANCE OF STUDYING TYPOGRAPHY

Typography is a crucial aspect of graphic design that greatly impacts a design's visual appeal and effectiveness. You must study typography and type's anatomy to be able to understand and become good at it, as it is a visual language that enables communication, expresses emotions, structures information, reflects cultural influences, and fosters universal understanding through visual elements and design principles. According to Ellen Lupton, author of *Thinking With Type*: **"Typography is what language looks like."**

Here are some tips for a beginning graphic designer looking to enhance your typography skills;

Understand the Basics: Familiarize yourself with typography terms like *serif* and *sans-serif* fonts, *kerning, leading, tracking*, and *hierarchy*. Knowing these terms will help you communicate effectively and understand design principles.

Choose Fonts Wisely: Select fonts that align with the design's purpose and tone. Consider readability and legibility, especially for body text. Try experimenting with font pairings to create visual interest while maintaining coherence.

Hierarchy Matters: Establish a clear typographic hierarchy by varying font sizes, weights, and styles. Headings, subheadings, and body text should have distinct visual differences to guide attention and convey information effectively.

Pay Attention to Alignment: Ensure proper alignment of text elements. Left, right, center, or justified alignments all have their uses, but consistency within a design is crucial for a polished and professional look.

Mind the White Space: Embrace white space to enhance readability and visual appeal. Provide enough space around text elements to prevent crowding and allow breathing room for comfortable navigation.

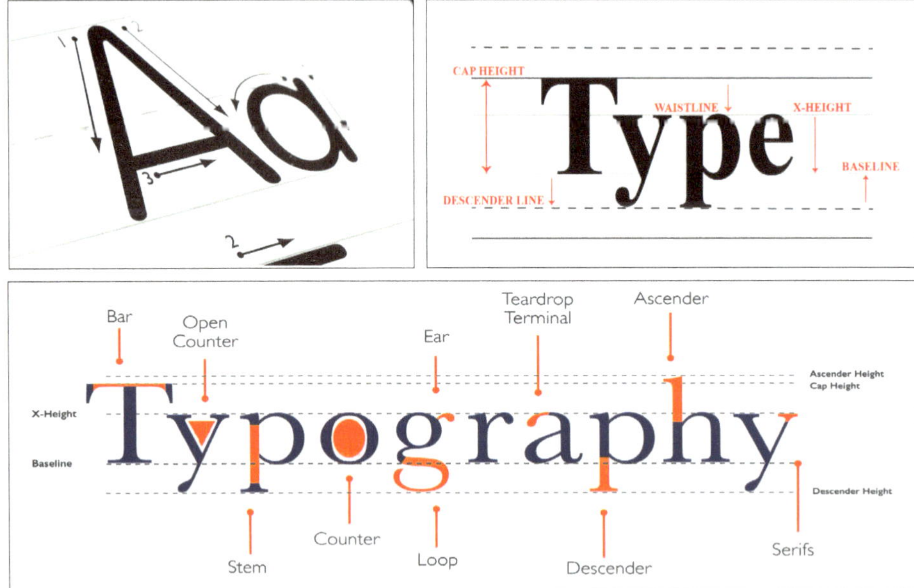

It is important to study and understand the anatomy of letterforms. Understanding the anatomy of letterforms is essential for achieving consistency, and mastery in typography

TYPE CATEGORIES

Type can be classified into two categories:

SERIFS/SANS SERIF

SERIF: Garamond, Baskerville, Didot
SANS SERIF: Helvetica, Arial, Gill Sans

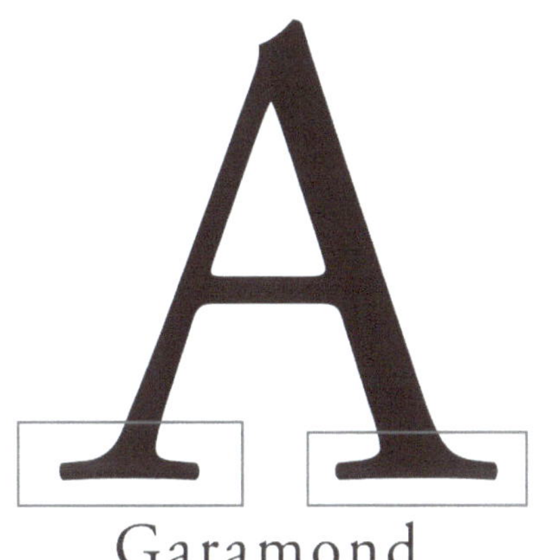
Garamond

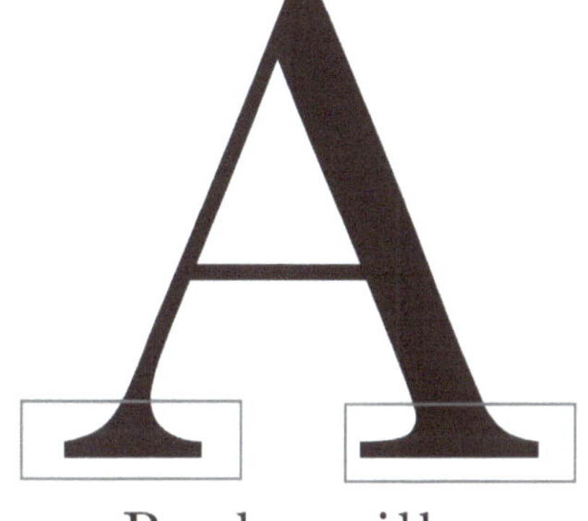
Baskerville

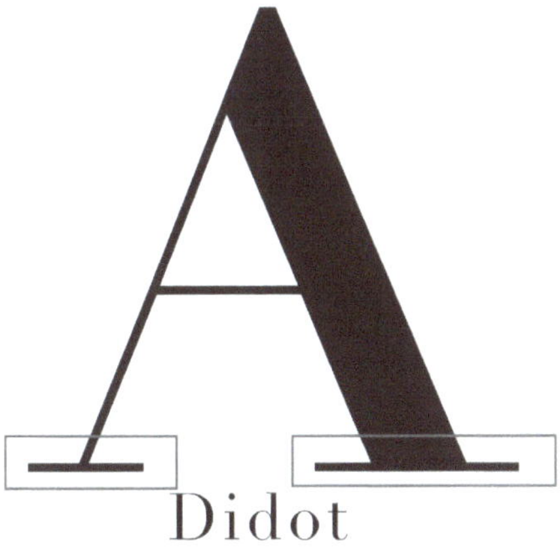
Didot

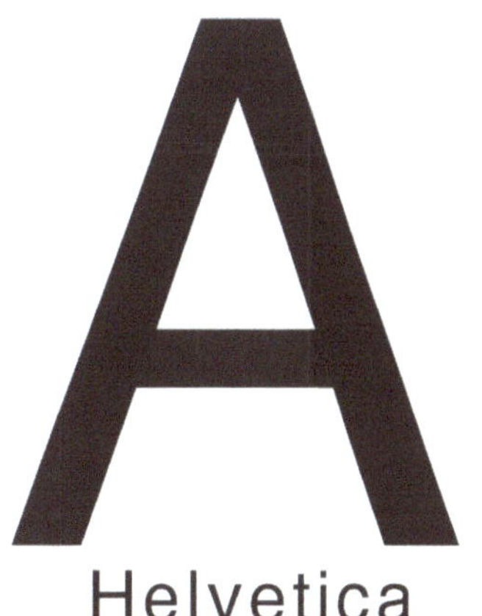
Helvetica

Serif and sans-serif are typefaces distinguished by the presence or absence of small finishing strokes, referred to as "serifs." These strokes are the decorative details or feet at the ends of the characters.

A fun typography class project on type anatomy

The main objective of the project was to convey the anatomy of type as clearly as possible and in a visually interesting way on three cubes each measuring 6 inches, 5 inches, and 4 inches. Each cube should appear as part of a series, created in Adobe Illustrator, and should visually explain the anatomical terms to someone new to the subject. All six sides of the cubes must be used, with no more than three of the provided terms on each side.

Use any serif or sans serif typeface, upper and/or lowercase only. Students could enlarge/reduce, crop/cut out sections, or anything that helped explain the terms to the viewer. The designs could be as dramatic as possible, while still maintaining legibility and readability.

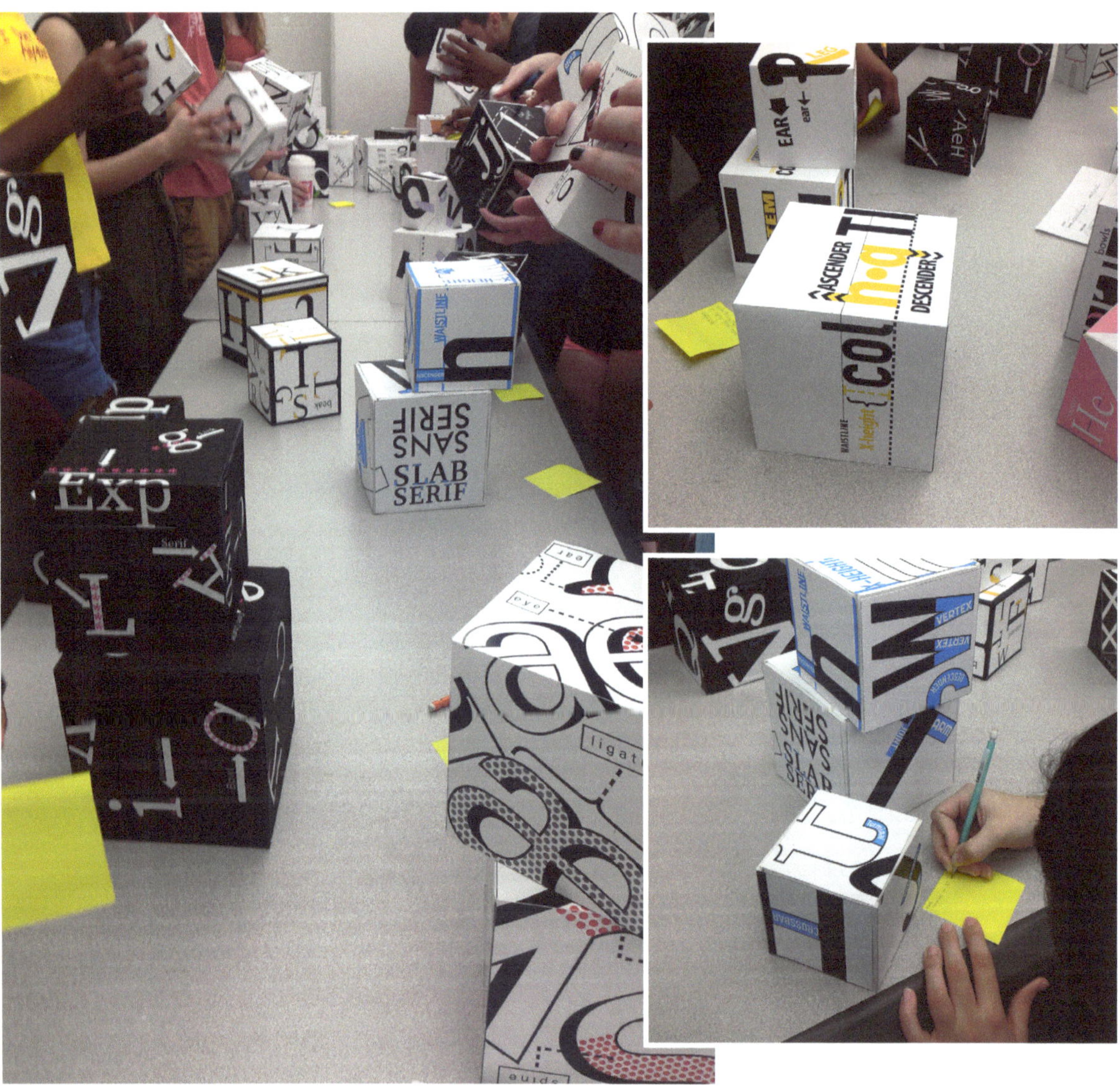

After the design and construction of their individual cubes, students were tasked with the review and critique of each other's cubes to determine whether the creations met the criteria, were well-crafted, and the terms were correctly identified, legible, and readable. Embracing the critique and being open to feedback are integral parts of the design journey and could help identify potential issues or challenges in a design before its final refinement.

Experiment with creative typography

To enhance your creativity with letterforms, it is important to explore and experiment with various styles, shapes, and arrangements of letters. Develop your own letterforms or modify existing ones to create a unique typographic expression. Create an ornate or decorative letterform just for fun or to use as a drop cap at the beginning of a paragraph. Look for letters in the environment, and create an alphabet out of found items, they're there, you just have to train your mind to look for them. This can be creative and fun!

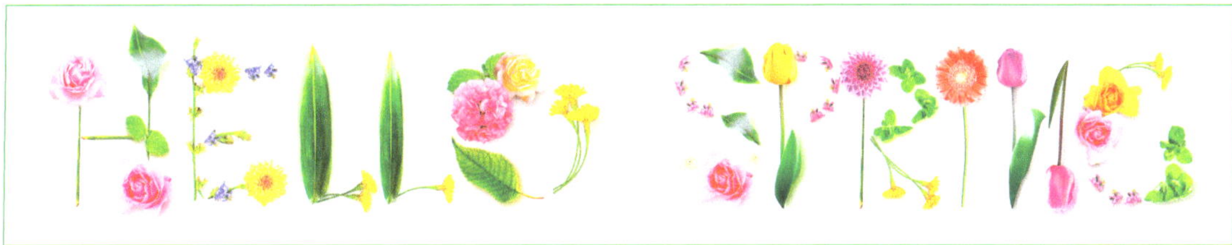

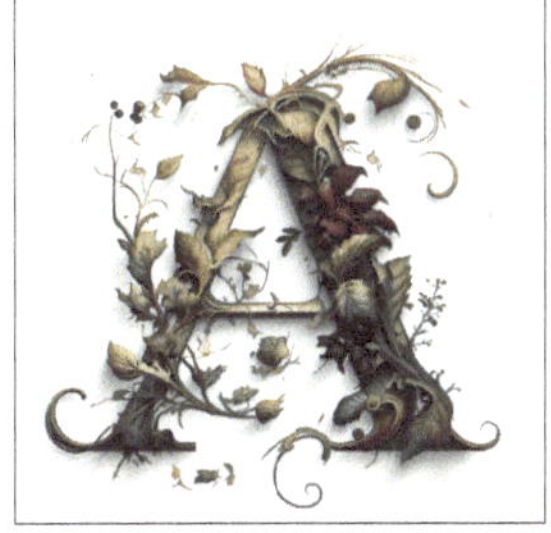

Incorporate Illustrations: Combine letterforms with illustrations or graphics to create a cohesive and visually interesting design. This integration can add depth and complexity to your lettering.

Pair Fonts Thoughtfully: When combining fonts, consider their compatibility. Aim for contrast between fonts (e.g., pairing a sans-serif with a serif font) while ensuring a harmonious overall look. Avoid using too many fonts in a single design.

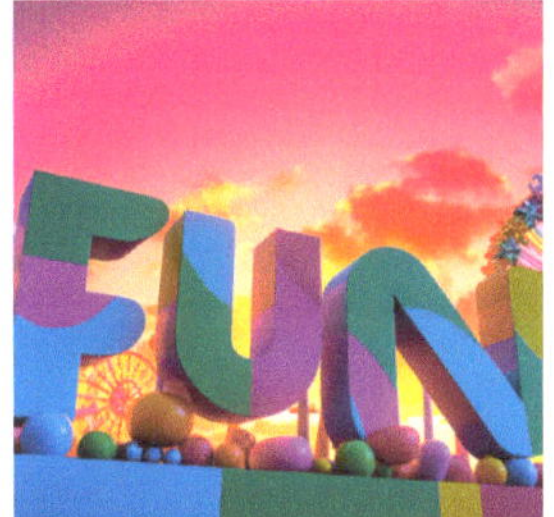

Embrace Different Mediums: Use different mediums such as ink, watercolor, chalk, or digital tools to create your letterforms. Each medium has its unique characteristics that can influence the style and texture of your designs.

Draw Inspiration From Different Sources: Look for inspiration in diverse places, such as nature, architecture, art, and even everyday objects. Drawing connections between unrelated concepts can lead to unique and innovative lettering ideas.

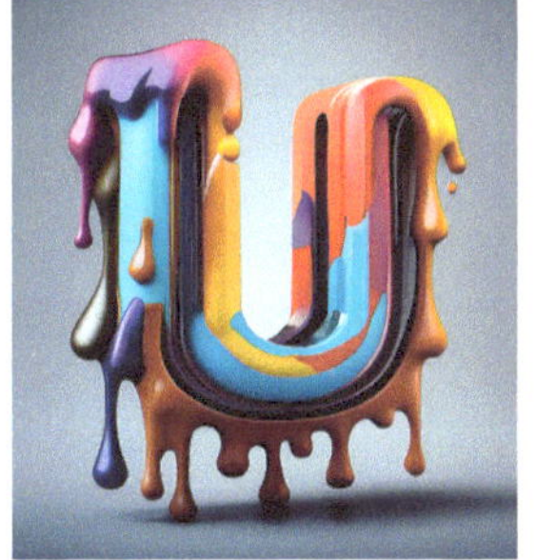

Get Feedback and Refine: Seek feedback from peers or mentors to gain insights into your typography choices. Use constructive feedback to refine your skills and continuously improve your designs.

Study Typography in the Wild: Observe well-designed materials like books, magazines, websites, billboards, street signs, and advertisements. Analyze and study how professional designers use typography to convey messages effectively.

Remember, mastering typography is an ongoing process, and practice is key. Continuously explore new fonts, experiment with different layouts, and stay informed about evolving design trends to enhance your typography skills over time. Always engage in the critique of your designs before finalization of projects.

THE IMPORT AND VALUE OF
THE DESIGN CRITIQUE

A design critique is extremely valuable at different stages of the design process. It is usually conducted in a structured manner to maximize productivity, effectiveness, and alignment with the design brief.

Here are the key steps involved in conducting a design critique:

Preparation:

• Select a convenient time and place for the critique that works for all participants.
• Gather all necessary materials, such as design mockups, prototypes, or sketches, that will be reviewed during the critique.
• Determine the focus and goals of the critique. What aspects of the design do you want feedback on? What specific questions do you want to address?

Introduction:

• Begin the critique by introducing the design and providing context. Explain the project goals, target audience, and any relevant constraints or considerations.
• Clarify the purpose of the critique and set expectations for participation. Emphasize the importance of constructive feedback and respectful communication.

Presentation:

• The designer presents the design to the group, walking through key elements, features, and design decisions. This presentation should be concise but thorough, highlighting the main aspects of the design.
• Encourage the designer to explain their design rationale, user considerations, and any specific areas where they are seeking feedback.

Feedback and Discussion:

• Open the floor for feedback and discussion. Encourage participants to share their thoughts, impressions, and suggestions for improvement.
• Focus the discussion on specific aspects of the design, such as usability, visual aesthetics, information architecture, or functionality.
• Ensure that feedback is constructive, specific, and actionable. Avoid personal criticism and focus on the design itself.
• Encourage a diversity of perspectives and viewpoints. Different participants may have unique insights based on their backgrounds, expertise, or experiences.

Facilitation:

• As the facilitator, guide the discussion and keep it on track. Ensure that everyone has an opportunity to speak and that the conversation remains focused on the design objectives.
• Manage the time effectively to allow for thorough feedback without exceeding the allotted time.

Conclusion:

- Summarize the key points discussed during the critique.
- Allow the designer to ask any follow-up questions or seek clarification on the feedback received.
- Express appreciation to all participants for their contributions and engagement.

Follow-Up:

- After the critique, the designer can incorporate feedback into the design and make revisions as needed.
- Consider scheduling follow-up critiques to review the updated design and track progress.

Here are some key reasons why design critiques hold significance:

Feedback and Improvement: Design critiques offer designers the opportunity to receive constructive feedback from peers, mentors, or clients. This feedback helps identify strengths and weaknesses in the design, provides fresh perspectives, and suggests improvements. By incorporating critique feedback, designers can refine their work and produce more effective designs.

Validation and Challenge: Design critiques can validate design decisions or challenge assumptions. They help ensure that design choices align with project goals, user needs, and design principles. By discussing and defending design decisions during critiques, designers can strengthen their rationale and build confidence in their work.

Learning and Growth: Participating in design critiques exposes designers to diverse viewpoints and approaches. It fosters a culture of learning, collaboration, and continuous improvement within design teams or communities. Designers can learn from each other's successes and failures, gain new insights, and broaden their design skills and knowledge.

Communication Skills: Presenting and discussing designs during critiques hones communication skills. Designers learn to articulate their design intentions, receive and interpret feedback effectively, and engage in productive discussions with stakeholders. These communication skills are essential for conveying design concepts, collaborating with team members, and advocating for design decisions.

Building Relationships: Design critiques foster a sense of community and camaraderie among designers. They provide opportunities for networking, building relationships, and establishing trust and respect within design teams or communities. Designers can bond over shared experiences, support each other's growth, and create a supportive environment for creativity and innovation.

Overall, design critiques play a crucial role in the design process by facilitating feedback, promoting learning and growth, enhancing communication skills, and fostering a sense of community. They contribute to the development of high-quality, user-centered designs and empower designers to create impactful solutions. By following these steps, a design critique can provide valuable insights, foster collaboration, and ultimately improve the quality of the design.

A research project on exploring typographic grid systems

The typographic systems are similar to what architects call "shape grammars" and they are a part of graphic design studies. Traditionally, many designers focus on using traditional grid systems for designs based on a vertical column structure. However, in a beginning typography course, students studied and explored other variations of the grid outside of the traditional structure. These variations included axial, radial, dilatational, random, modular, bilateral, and transitional grids, as described in Kimberly Elam's book on *Typographic Systems.* Designs were limited to black and one other color.

The main objective of the project was to develop variations of the systems, each in an 8" square, using given text related to submitting a portfolio to the Graphic Communication concentration at Kennesaw State University. One creative traditional grid on a well-known designer was also assigned.

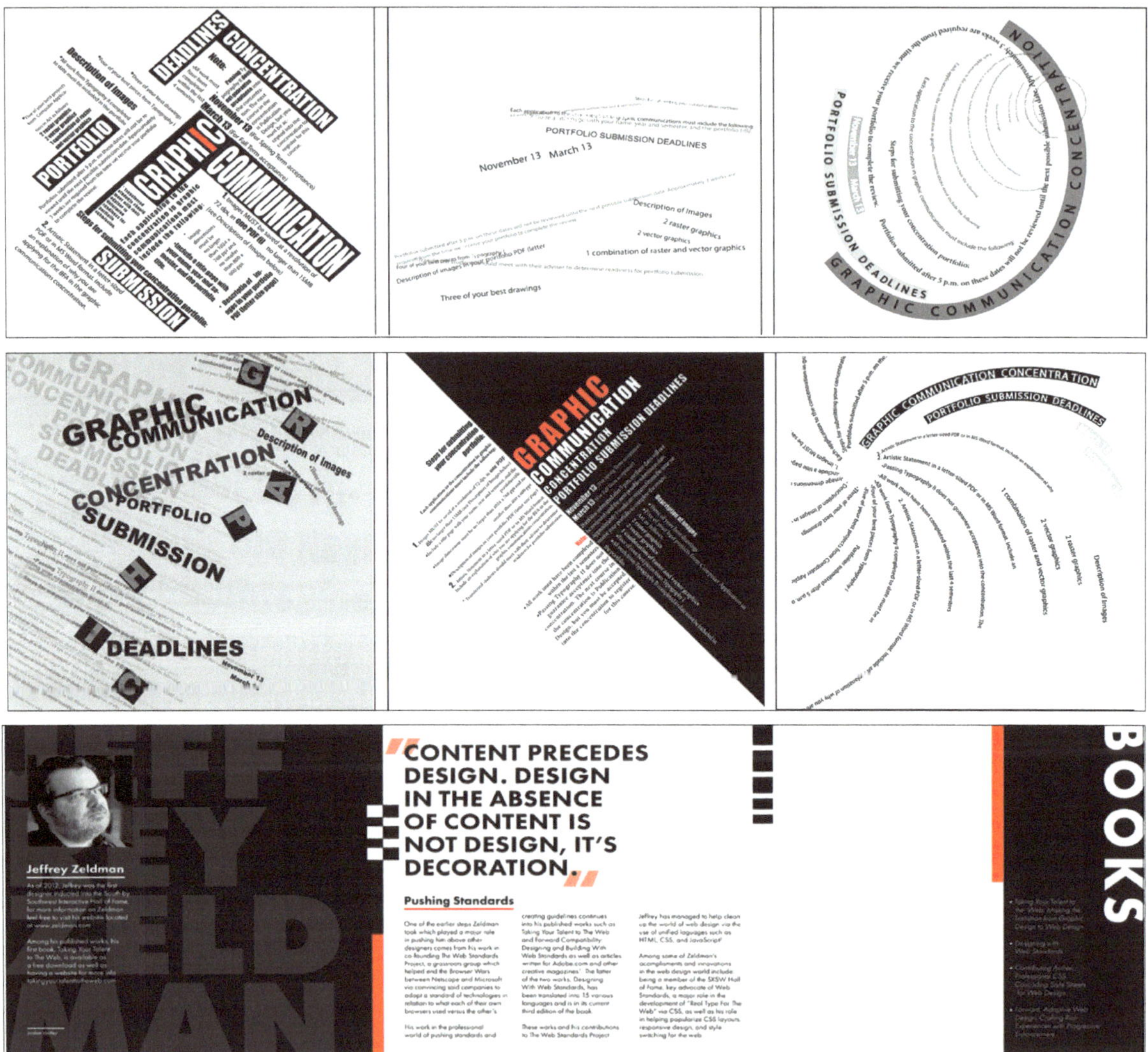

Top: Explorations of six of the *Typographic Systems.*
Student Designer: *Preston Luk / Kennesaw State University.*

Below: A creative solution using a traditional grid highlighting the well known designer, Jeffrey Zeldman.
Student Designer: *Jordan Costley / Kennesaw State University.*

A research project on a notable graphic designer

Researching and studying the work of notable graphic designers are valuable sources of learning and inspiration for graphic design students. It not only helps to enhance their technical skills but also contributes to their creative development, industry knowledge, and professional growth. Each graphic designer has a unique style and technique, and by studying the work of different designers, students are able to gain a deeper understanding and appreciation for various design styles, ranging from minimalist to ornate, as well as different techniques for visual communication.

The main goal of this project was to research and select a reputable graphic designer whose style and approach aligned with the students' preferences. The students would carefully analyze the chosen designer's work, focusing on their problem-solving techniques, and historical influences. Furthermore, students would explore their use of typography and design aesthetics. Ultimately, the students would present their research findings in a six-panel brochure. Students were encouraged to utilize white space in their design.

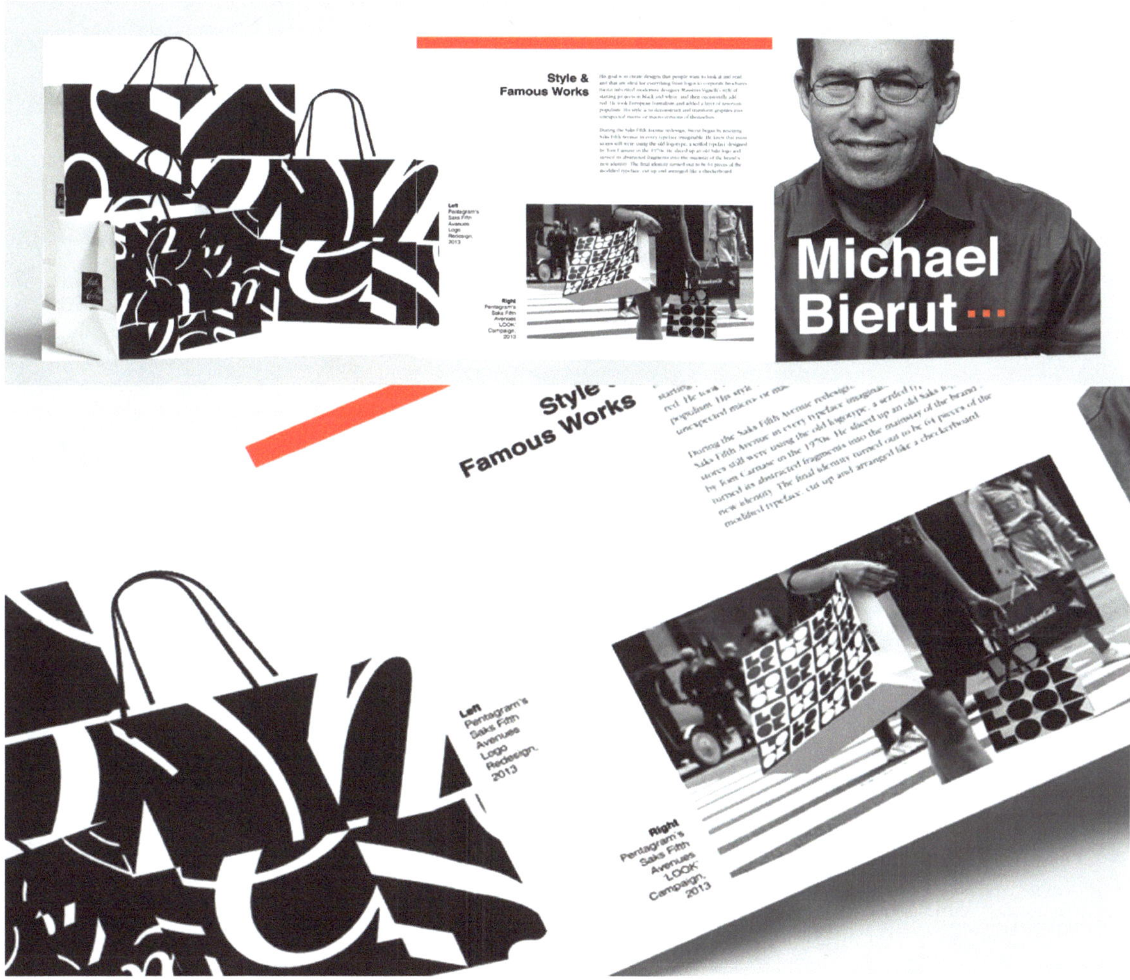

A Six-Panel brochure on the well-known graphic designer, Michael Beirut.
Student Designer: *Sally (Yeseul) Cho / Kennesaw State University.*

THE SIGNIFICANCE OF COLOR IN DESIGN AND BRANDING

Color in design and branding

Color is a crucial element in design and branding, playing a significant role in shaping perceptions, creating recognition, and influencing consumer behavior.

Several key reasons highlighting the importance of color in branding:

Brand Recognition:
Consistent color usage builds a strong brand identity, offering a visual cue for instant recognition among consumers.

Emotional Impact:
Colors evoke emotions and influence how a brand is perceived. Each color carries psychological associations, allowing brands to convey specific feelings. For instance, blue signifies trust, while red evokes excitement.

Memorability:
Distinctive color schemes help brands be memorable. Consistent colors create a lasting impression and enhance brand recall.

Differentiation:
Unique colors help brands stand out in competitive markets, aiding visual differentiation, and brand identification.

Brand Personality:
Colors define a brand's personality and traits, reflecting whether it is modern, traditional, playful, or serious.

Cultural Relevance:
Colors have cultural meanings. Brands must be mindful of cultural nuances to ensure chosen colors resonate positively with diverse audiences.

Communication:
Colors convey messages effectively, especially in today's diverse, visually-driven digital world.

Consistency:
Maintaining color consistency across platforms is essential for a unified brand presence and identity.

Perception:
Colors influence product and service perceptions, indicating quality and service levels.

Decision-Making:
Color impacts consumer buying decisions by attracting the target audience and creating positive brand associations. Strategic color usage in branding is more than just aesthetics; it is a powerful tool for creating a unique identity, fostering emotional connections with consumers, and influencing brand success and hence consumer purchase.

Color in mockups and design marketplace

Color Palette Generators:

Platforms like Coolors or Adobe Color Wheel are places where you can explore and discover color palettes. Use these palettes as a starting point for your mockup projects.

Typography and Font Pairing Sites:

Websites like Google Fonts or Typ.io showcase font pairings. Use these pairings to inspire mockup designs that complement specific typography choices.

Envato Elements:

Offers a wide range of design assets, including mockups. Browse their collection to discover different styles and use cases.

Creative Market:

A marketplace for various design resources, including mockup templates. Explore the diverse options available for inspiration.

Design Blogs and Magazines:

Follow design blogs and online magazines like *Smashing Magazine, Creative Bloq,* or *UX Design* for inspiration articles, showcases, and tutorials on creating effective mockups.

Social Media Platforms:

Pinterest: Create mood boards and pin mockup ideas that catch your eye. Pinterest is an excellent platform for collecting visual inspiration.

Instagram: Follow design accounts and hashtags to discover innovative mockups and designers' presentation styles.

Branding and Design Awards:

Explore branding and design award websites like the AIGA Design Awards, GDUSA Design Awards, 48 HR REPACK— Student Design Awards, Communication Arts, or Red Dot Awards. Winning projects often feature outstanding mockup presentations.

Behaviors in Real Life:

Observe packaging, signage, and advertisements in your daily surroundings. Real-world examples can inspire unique and practical mockup ideas.

User Interface (UI) Kits and Templates:

Explore UI kits available on platforms like Sketch App Sources or Figma Community. These kits often include pre-designed elements that can spark ideas for your mockups.

AI-generated color wheels

Color wheels are visual tools that arrange colors based on their chromatic relationships. They are generally presented as a circular diagram that illustrates the relationships between colors that are commonly utilized in art, design, and other visual fields to comprehend color harmony and connections. The concept of "AI Generated Color Wheels" implies that artificial intelligence (AI) plays a role in producing color schemes.

AI applications and tools exist to aid in generating and suggesting colors according to different factors like color theory, user preferences, or current designs. These tools analyze extensive datasets of color combinations and patterns to offer recommendations for visually appealing color schemes.

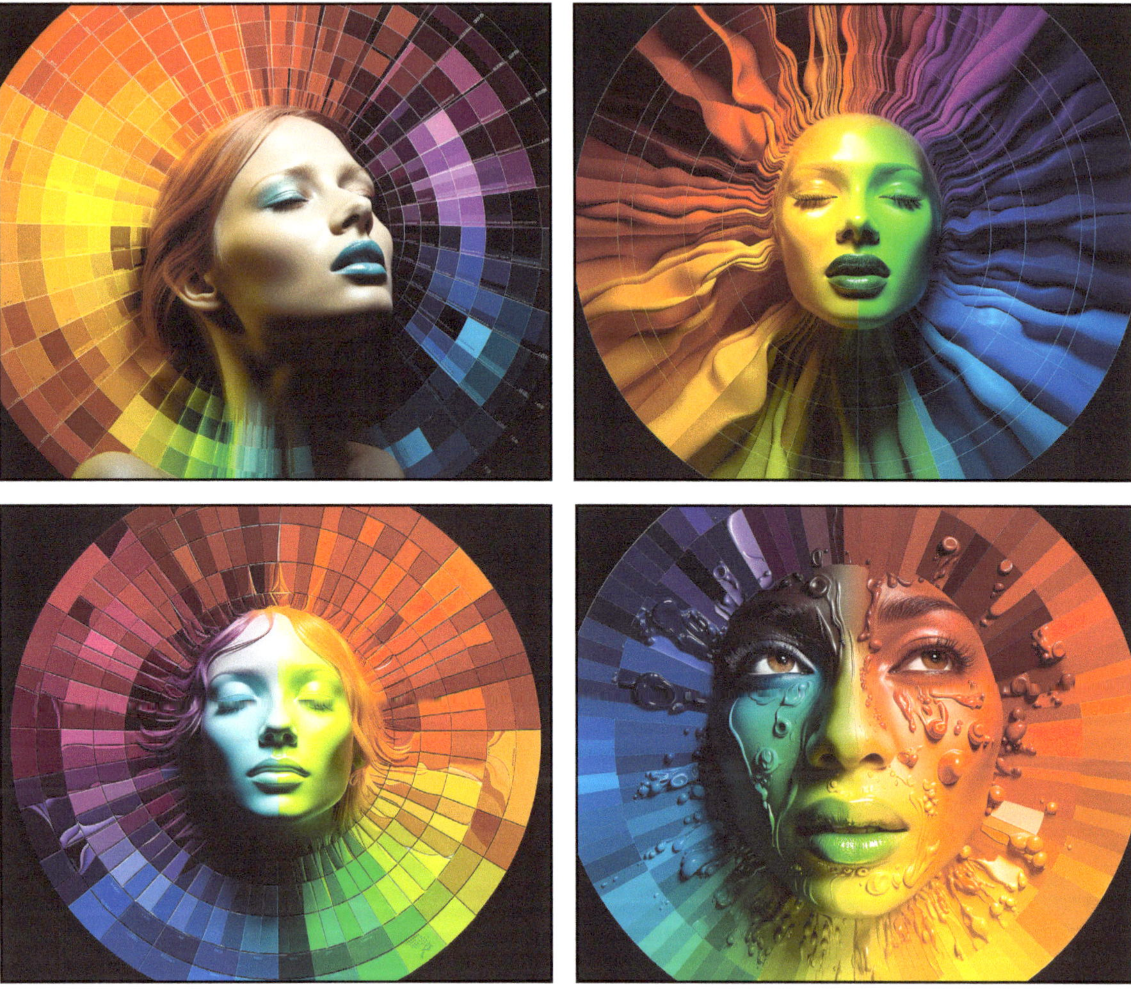

These color wheels are AI generated faces showcasing a spectrum of emotions, arranged to each look like a color wheel. Color wheels categorize colors according to their chromatic properties, which aids in comprehending color harmony and combinations. The standard color wheel includes primary colors (red, blue, and yellow), secondary colors (green, orange, and purple), and tertiary colors (created by mixing a primary and a secondary color). While the placement of colors on the wheel may differ, it generally represents their visual connections, rendering it a valuable tool in art, design, and color theory.

Explore color palettes & color schemes for design and branding inspiration

To explore color palettes outside of color generators and AI models, visit your hardware stores such as The Home Depot, Lowe's, Sherwin Williams or others, to browse paint chips. Some will allow you to take samples. Explore the outdoors to discover stunning nature-inspired color combinations. Cosmetic and nail polish counters also offer vibrant hues for inspiration. Image banks are some of the best resources to peruse and explore color palettes. Use color wheels to experiment with different schemes, like primary, secondary, triadic, and analogous combinations.

Analyze how competitors or industry leaders present their products or services. While not directly copying, understanding successful approaches can inform your mockup design strategies.

Remember that inspiration can come from various sources, and it's essential to blend different ideas to create something unique. Keep an open mind, experiment with different styles, and adapt elements that resonate with your project's goals and target audience.

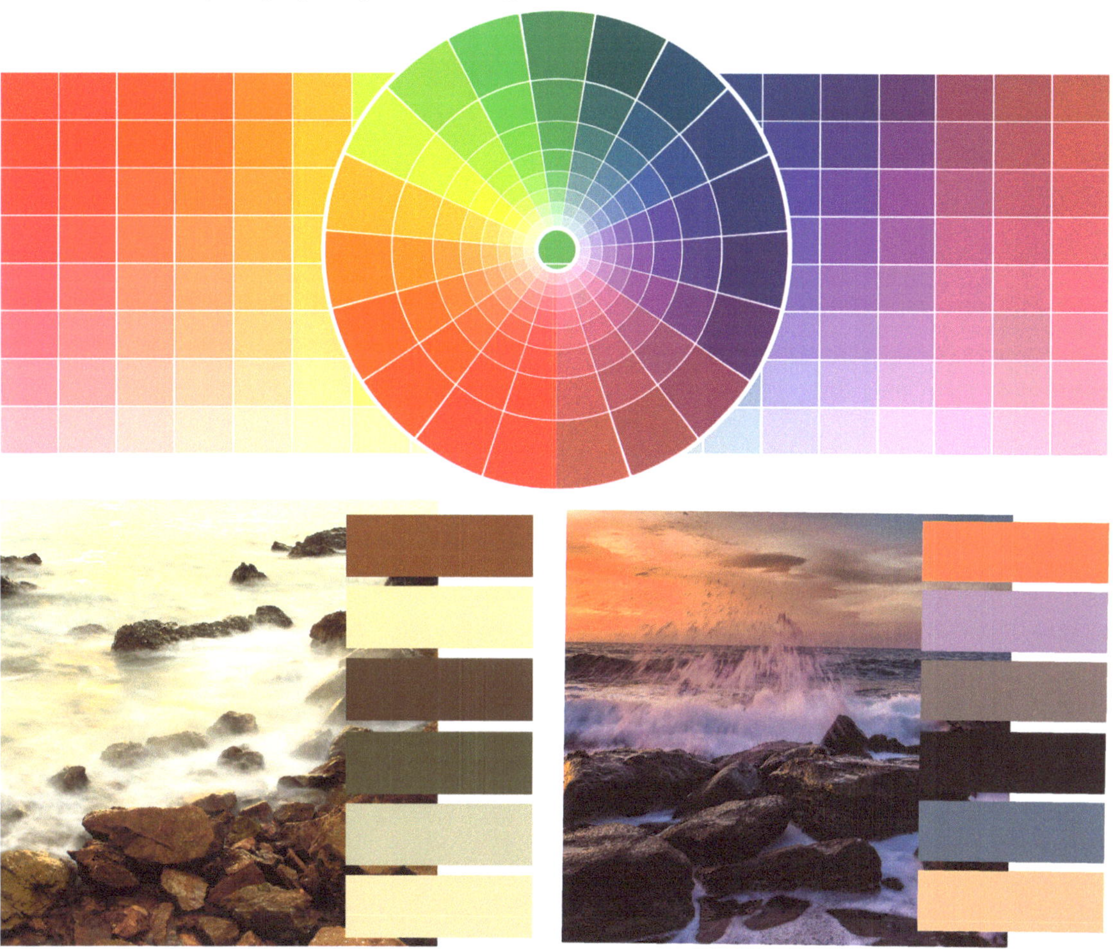

Above: *A traditional styled color wheel.*

Below: *All natural color palettes drawn from nature. To the left is a neutral seascape with rocks at sunrise. To the right is a stunning seascape at sunset. A color palette can be drawn from any image, and sometimes can help provide visual cohesiveness in a design.*

RGB and CMYK Color Models

RGB (Red, Green, Blue) and CMYK (Cyan, Magenta, Yellow, Black) are two different color models used in various contexts, particularly in digital and print media.

These are the key differences between RGB and CMYK:

Primary Colors:

RGB: Uses additive color mixing, combining red, green, and blue light to create a broad spectrum of colors. The more light you add, the closer you get to white.

CMYK: Uses subtractive color mixing, combining cyan, magenta, yellow, and black ink. The more color you add, the closer you get to black.

Color Representation:

RGB: Primarily used for electronic displays such as computer monitors, television screens, and digital cameras. It is the color model used in digital media, websites, photography, and applications where colors are displayed on a screen.

CMYK: Primarily used for color printing, including magazines, brochures, and other printed materials. Printers use these four ink colors in combination to reproduce a wide range of colors.

Color Gamut:

RGB: Has a larger color gamut, which means it can represent a broader range of colors, especially vibrant and bright hues. This is suitable for displays where the source of light is emitted.

CMYK: Has a more limited color gamut compared to RGB. It may struggle to reproduce certain bright and saturated colors accurately, which can be a consideration in print production.

Black Color:

RGB: The combination of the full intensity of red, green, and blue results in white. There is no dedicated black channel in RGB. However, if you pull the R, G and B sliders all down to 0 in your swatches panel, you effectively get black.

CMYK: Includes a dedicated black channel (K for Key) because combining the full intensity of cyan, magenta, and yellow often results in a muddy brown color. Adding black helps achieve a true black in print.

Remember that for high-quality printing, images should be saved at a resolution of 300 pixels per inch (ppi) or higher. Use the CMYK color mode for color printing to guarantee accurate color reproduction. Use the RGB color mode for onscreen and for digital devices. The optimal onscreen resolution is typically 72 ppi, but this can vary depending on the context and use.

NOTABLE CONTRIBUTIONS FROM
COLOR THEORISTS

Certain individuals have made notable contributions to understanding and applying color in graphic design. These color theorists have established the foundation for our comprehension of color in design, including the fundamentals of the color wheel and the psychological effects of color choices. Their works still influence how designers use color in different creative fields.

Five renowned figures in color theory along with some of their notable works:

Johannes Itten:

Notable Works:
The Art of Color (book)
Developed the color wheel used in art and design education
Taught at the Bauhaus School and influenced its color theory curriculum

Albert Munsell:

Notable Works:
Munsell Color System
A Color Notation (book)
Developed a three-dimensional color model, the Munsell color space

Josef Albers:

Notable Works:
Interaction of Color (book)
Homage to the Square series of paintings
Taught color theory at the Bauhaus and Black Mountain College

Faber Birren:

Notable Works:
Color Psychology and Color Therapy (book)
Extensive research on the psychological effects of color
Contributed to the understanding of color in marketing and branding

M.E. Chevreul:

Notable Works:
The Principles of Harmony and Contrast of Colors (book)
Explored the principles of simultaneous contrast
Influential in the development of color theory in the 19th century

Image file formats for print and online

There are several image file types commonly used for both print and online purposes, each with its own characteristics and advantages. When preparing images for print, it's important to use high-resolution files (usually 300 dpi or higher) to ensure quality. For online use, consider the balance between file size and image quality to optimize loading times on web pages.

These are some of the most common file types:

JPEG (Joint Photographic Experts Group):

Print: JPEGs are suitable for print, especially in situations where file size needs to be minimized. However, it's essential to save them with high quality and minimal compression to avoid loss of detail.
Online: JPEGs are widely used for online images, as they provide a good balance between file size and image quality. They are suitable for photographs and images with gradients.

PNG (Portable Network Graphics):

Print: PNGs are suitable for print when the image has a transparent background or when lossless compression is required. They are commonly used for logos and graphics with sharp edges.
Online: PNGs are commonly used for online graphics, icons, logos, and images that require transparency. They support lossless compression.

TIFF (Tagged Image File Format):

Print: TIFFs are a popular choice for print because they support lossless compression and store high-quality images. They are commonly used in professional printing processes.
Online: TIFFs are rarely used online due to their large file sizes.

GIF (Graphics Interchange Format):

Print: GIFs are not typically used for print due to their limited color palette (256 colors). They are not suitable for high-quality images.
Online: GIFs are commonly used for simple animations, icons, and images with a limited color palette. They support transparency.

SVG (Scalable Vector Graphics):

Print: SVGs are vector graphics suitable for print when scalability is essential. They can be resized without losing quality.
Online: SVGs are widely used for online graphics, logos, and icons. They are lightweight and support scalability.

PDF (Portable Document Format):

Print: While not an image format per se, PDFs can embed images and are widely used for print documents, especially when preserving formatting and layout is crucial.
Online: PDFs are also used for online documents and presentations.

The History Behind PDF:

The Portable Document Format (PDF) was developed by Adobe Systems, a software company founded by John Warnock and Charles Geschke. The idea for PDF originated in the early 1990s when Warnock, who was Adobe's co-founder and chief architect, envisioned a universal document format that would preserve the look and feel of documents across different computer systems and printers.

PDF was officially introduced in 1993, and the first version was released by Adobe Acrobat software. The format was designed to address the challenges of sharing documents across different platforms and printing devices without losing formatting or layout. PDF achieved this by encapsulating text, fonts, images, and other elements in a self-contained file that could be reliably reproduced on various devices.

Several factors contribute to the widespread adoption of PDF:

Cross-Platform Compatibility: PDFs can be viewed and printed consistently across different operating systems, including Windows, macOS, and Linux. This makes it a reliable choice for document exchange.

Document Integrity: PDFs are designed to maintain the integrity of the document's layout, fonts, and images. This is especially important for professional and legal documents where the visual presentation is crucial.

Security Features: PDFs can be password-protected, encrypted, and have other security features, making them suitable for sensitive and confidential information.

Interactive Elements: PDFs support interactive elements such as hyperlinks, forms, and multimedia content, enhancing their versatility for a variety of purposes.

Printability: PDFs are designed to be printable, ensuring that documents can be reproduced on paper with high fidelity to the original digital version.

Archival Stability: PDF/A, a subset of the PDF standard, is specifically designed for the long-term preservation of electronic documents. It ensures that documents will remain readable and accessible in the future.

The open standardization of PDF by the International Organization for Standardization (ISO) in 2008 (ISO 32000-1:2008) further contributed to its widespread use. Today, PDF is a ubiquitous format for sharing documents, and it is widely used in various industries for creating, distributing, and archiving digital documents.

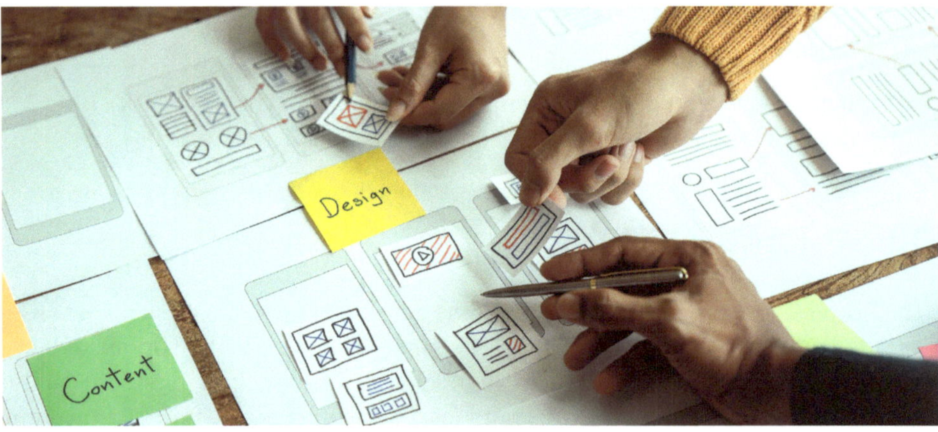

Designers share thumbnails (a quick visual view of their ideas, not meant to be finished concepts) and discuss design and content to solve the problem.

The design process is crucial in graphic design. It plays a fundamental role in creating effective communication materials. Designers follow a series of systematic steps to achieve this goal. Here are some main reasons why the design process is important in graphic design and what it includes:

Understanding the Client's Brief:
• **Client Interaction and Collaboration:** Designers meet with clients to understand project requirements, goals, and constraints, to ensure that the final product will align with the client's vision and objectives. This collaboration is essential for client satisfaction and project success.
• **Research:** Designers gather information about target audiences, competitors, industry trends, and other relevant factors based on the client's brief.

Conceptualization and What Ifs:
• **What if Sessions:** These brainstorming sessions are crucial for fostering creativity and innovation. They involve exploring hypothetical scenarios and possibilities, allowing participants to break free from their usual thought patterns and challenge assumptions. This approach can lead to unexpected breakthrough insights, helping teams discover fresh approaches and push the boundaries of what is possible, ultimately enhancing the quality and diversity of generated ideas.
• **Sketching:** Designers develop thumbnails or rough concepts on paper to visualize and refine ideas.

Design Development:
• **Digital Design:** Designers create digital versions of their concepts using graphic design software.
• **Mockups:** Designers develop mockups or prototypes to provide a realistic representation of the final design.

Feedback and Refinement:
• **Client Feedback:** Designers gather feedback from clients to refine and improve the design. Designers can revisit and adjust their work based on feedback and changing requirements, allowing for continuous improvement and adaptation.

HOW IMPORTANT IS THE DESIGN PROCESS?

Finalization:
- **Approval:** Designers seek final approval from clients or stakeholders.
- **Refinement:** They fine-tune and make last-minute adjustments to meet all requirements.

Production and Implementation:
- **Preparation for Print or Digital:** Designers prepare the final files for printing or digital distribution.
- **Collaboration with Production Teams:** They work with printers, developers, or other production teams if needed.

Delivery and Evaluation:
- **Delivery to Client:** The final design is delivered to the client or released for public consumption.
- **Evaluation:** Designers assess the success of the project through feedback, performance metrics, or post-project evaluations.

In summary, the design process is essential in graphic design as it provides a structured and systematic approach to problem-solving, fosters creativity, facilitates collaboration, ensures efficiency, promotes consistency, considers user experience, enhances communication, and allows for flexibility and adaptation.

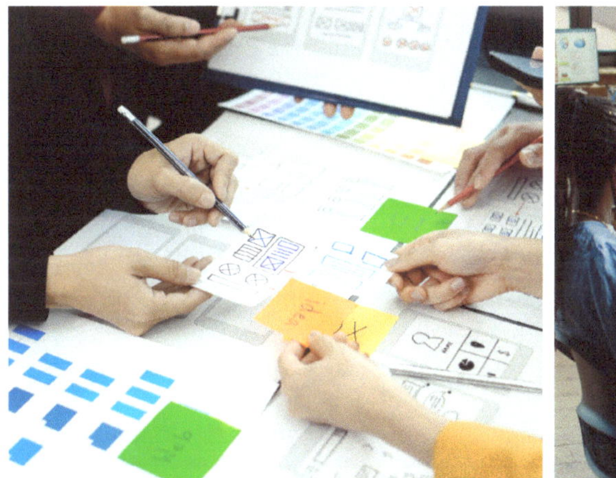

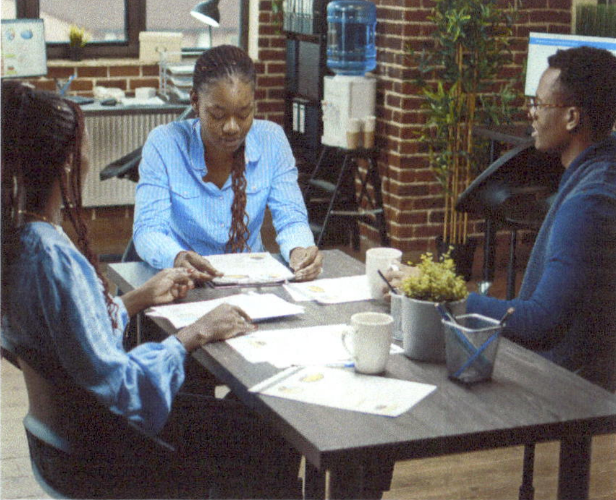

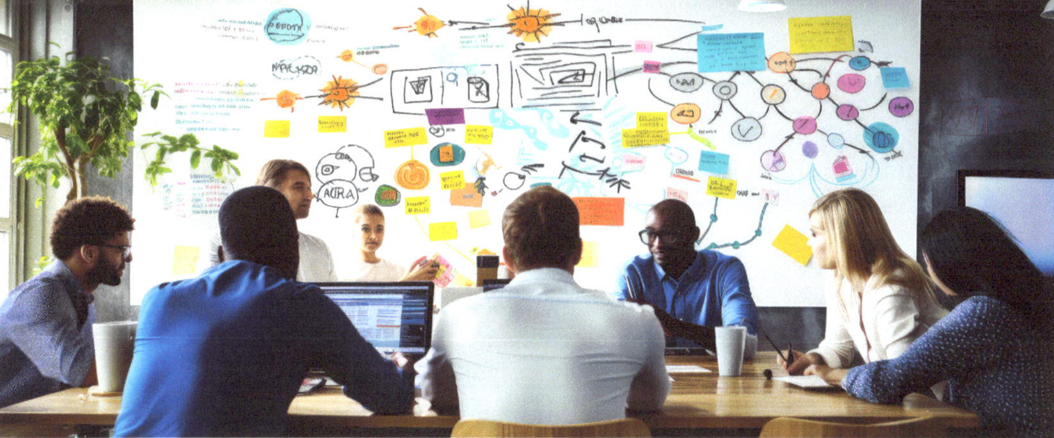

Three brainstorming groups/teams in action working to generate ideas and explore various directions for solving the design problems at hand. Instructors usually divide students into teams to brainstorming on design projects.

THE IMPORTANCE OF RESEARCH AND THUMBNAILS

The research and thumbnail phases in graphic design can vary among designers, depending on their process, project requirements, and their personal preferences. However, both research and thumbnails are crucial aspects of the design process and often occur simultaneously.

Designers may prioritize one over the other based on their individual process and project requirements, but both research and thumbnails play essential roles in the design process and often inform each other iteratively throughout the creative journey. Several projects' thumbnails can be seen alongside their mockups throghout the book.

Some designers prefer to begin the design process by conducting research in order to fully comprehend the project's objectives, target audience, context, and limitations. Research may include gathering information, analyzing the target audience, studying competitors, exploring design trends, and understanding the client's brand or message. Once the research is complete, designers proceed to explore visual concepts, layout ideas, and design solutions based on the insights gained from their research.

These are some common approaches:

Thumbnailing First, Research Second: Some designers may prefer to start the design process with thumbnail sketches as a way to generate ideas and explore visual concepts freely without being constrained by the findings of research. They brainstorm, experiment with different design elements, and quickly capture ideas on paper or digitally.

After generating a variety of thumbnail sketches, designers may then conduct research to inform and refine their initial concepts. The findings of the research may influence the direction of the design, the choice of visual elements, or the overall approach to the project.

Iterative Approach: Many designers adopt an iterative approach in which research and exploring thumbnails occur iteratively throughout the design process. Designers may start with initial research to establish a foundation for their designs, then move on to thumbnails to explore ideas and concepts.

As the design progresses, designers may conduct additional research to validate ideas, gather feedback, or address specific design challenges. Creating thumbnails continues alongside research, allowing designers to refine their designs based on new insights and findings.

Parallel Process: In some cases, research and thumbnail sketches may occur in parallel, with designers simultaneously conducting research while sketching ideas. As designers gather information and insights from their research, they may immediately translate those insights into visual concepts through thumbnails. This approach allows for a dynamic exchange between research and design, with each informing and influencing the other in real-time.

Why is Research so fundamental to the graphic design process?

Overall, research is essential to the graphic design process as it informs understanding, inspires creativity, guides problem-solving, informs decision-making, and ensures that ethical considerations are taken into account. By conducting research at various stages of the design process, designers can create designs that are impactful, relevant, and meaningful to their intended audience.

These are several reasons why doing research is important:

Understanding the Audience: Effective graphic design communicates with a specific audience. Research helps designers understand the demographics, preferences, behaviors, and needs of the target audience. By conducting audience research, designers can tailor their designs to resonate with the intended audience, resulting in more impactful and relevant visual communication.

Contextual Understanding: Researching the context in which a design will be used is crucial for creating effective solutions. Whether designing for a specific industry, cultural group, or geographic region, understanding the context helps designers create designs that are appropriate, culturally sensitive, and aligned with the goals of the project.

Inspiration and Innovation: Research serves as a source of inspiration and fuel for creativity. By exploring a wide range of sources such as art history, contemporary design trends, cultural movements, and technological advancements, designers can gain new perspectives, discover innovative ideas, and push the boundaries of their creativity.

Problem Solving: Graphic design often involves solving complex problems. Research helps designers gather information, analyze data, and identify insights that inform the design process. Whether it's understanding user needs, addressing usability issues, or solving communication challenges, research provides the foundation for effective problem-solving.

Visual Language and Semiotics: Researching visual language, semiotics, and design principles helps designers understand how visual elements like color, typography, imagery, and layout are perceived and interpreted by audiences. By studying the principles of design, designers can create designs that effectively communicate messages, evoke emotions, and convey meaning.

Competitive Analysis: Researching competitors and industry trends helps designers understand the competitive landscape and identify opportunities for differentiation. By analyzing competitors' designs, branding strategies, and marketing tactics, designers can develop designs that stand out, resonate with the target audience, and effectively communicate the client's unique value proposition.

Ethical Considerations: Research also plays a role in ethical decision-making in graphic design. Designers must consider ethical implications related to issues such as cultural sensitivity, representation, accessibility, and sustainability. Conducting thorough research helps designers make informed decisions and create designs that are ethical, inclusive, and socially responsible.

Where do graphic designers get inspiration from?

Graphic designers draw inspiration from various sources to fuel their creativity and inform their design process. These sources can include nature, art, technology, and culture. By exploring and synthesizing different influences, designers can create unique and meaningful designs that resonate with audiences and leave a lasting impact.

Some common sources of inspiration for graphic designers include:

Nature: Graphic designers can find inspiration in the natural forms, patterns, colors, and textures found in the environment. Drawing from landscapes, plants, animals, and natural phenomena can help create visually engaging designs with an organic feel.

Art and Art History: Works of art from different artistic movements, periods, and styles are rich sources of inspiration. Studying famous artists, such as painters, sculptors, and photographers, can provide insights into composition, color theory, and visual storytelling.

Typography and Lettering: Typography is a fundamental element of graphic design, and designers often find inspiration in the shapes, forms, and styles of letters and typefaces. Exploring historical typefaces, calligraphy, and lettering techniques can spark new ideas for typographic compositions.

Graphic Design History: Graphic designers frequently look to the past for inspiration, studying iconic designs, graphic movements, and design pioneers. Analyzing historical examples of graphic design can provide valuable insights into design principles, techniques, and trends.

Contemporary Design Trends: Staying up to date with current design trends and movements is essential for graphic designers seeking inspiration. Following design blogs, attending design conferences, and browsing design publications can expose designers to innovative techniques, styles, and approaches.

Technology and Innovation: Exploring new software features, emerging design trends, and innovative design techniques can inspire designers to push the boundaries of their creativity and the design landscape.

Cultural Influences: Designers may draw inspiration from cultural symbols, traditions, rituals, and aesthetics to create designs that resonate with specific audiences or communities.

Personal Experiences and Interests: Graphic designers draw from personal experiences and narratives, hobbies, passions, memories, and interests that infuse designs with authenticity, creativity, and emotional resonance.

Collaboration and Networking: Collaborating with other designers, creatives, and professionals can inspire new ideas and foster creativity. Engaging in design communities, attending workshops, and participating in collaborative projects can provide fresh perspectives.

Client Briefs and Project Requirements: Understanding the goals, objectives, and constraints of a design project can inspire designers to develop creative solutions that meet the client's needs and exceed expectations.

Sketching and generating thumbnails in the context of graphic design:

Sketching is a broad term that encompasses the act of creating rough drawings to explore ideas and concepts, while generating thumbnails specifically refers to creating small-scale sketches to explore multiple design options quickly and efficiently. Thumbnails are generally used in graphic design to generate and compare design iterations during the early stages of the design process. Graphic designers use thumbnails to explore ideas, concepts, and compositions during the early stages of the design process.

These thumbnails serve several important purposes:

Generating Ideas: Thumbnail sketches allow designers to generate a wide range of ideas quickly. By sketching out multiple variations and concepts in a short amount of time, designers can explore different directions and possibilities for their designs.

Exploring Composition: Thumbnail sketches help designers experiment with composition, layout, and arrangement of elements within a design. They can test different spatial relationships, proportions, and visual hierarchies to find the most effective arrangement for conveying the intended message or function.

Problem Solving: Thumbnail sketches facilitate problem-solving by allowing designers to visually brainstorm solutions to design challenges. Whether it's finding the best way to organize information, solve a usability issue, or communicate a complex idea, sketching provides a low-risk, iterative approach to experimentation.

Visual Communication: Thumbnail sketches serve as a form of visual communication, enabling designers to convey their ideas to others quickly and efficiently. These rough sketches can be shared with clients, collaborators, or team members to solicit feedback, generate discussion, and ensure alignment on design direction.

Iterative Design: Thumbnail sketches support an iterative design process, where designers can refine and iterate on their ideas based on feedback and reflection. By creating multiple iterations of thumbnail sketches, designers can progressively refine their designs, incorporating feedback and insights gained along the way.

Efficiency: Thumbnail sketches are a time-efficient way to explore ideas and concepts. They require minimal materials and can be created rapidly, allowing designers to explore numerous possibilities in a short amount of time without investing too much effort in any single concept.

Freedom and Creativity: Thumbnail sketches provide a space for creative exploration and experimentation. Since they are quick and informal, designers can feel free to take risks, explore unconventional ideas, and push the boundaries of their creativity without the fear of failure or judgment.

THE IMPORTANCE OF THE DESIGN LAYOUT

In graphic design, a layout is the arrangement and organization of visual elements on a page or screen. It involves strategically placing text, images, graphics, and other design elements to create a cohesive and visually appealing composition that effectively communicates a message or information to the audience. Layouts are essential for guiding the viewer's eye, conveying hierarchy and structure, and improving the readability and usability of a design.

Here are some key aspects of a layout in graphic design:

Composition refers to the overall structure and arrangement of design elements, including headers, body text, images, and other design components. Composition principles like balance, symmetry, alignment, and proximity are often applied to create visually pleasing and well-balanced layouts.

Hierarchy involves organizing content in a way that highlights certain elements over others, establishing a visual hierarchy that directs the viewer's attention. This is achieved through variations in size, color, contrast, and typography, emphasizing importance and sequence within the layout.

Whitespace, also known as negative space, is the use of empty space around elements to provide visual breathing room, enhance readability, and establish a sense of balance and harmony. Whitespace helps prevent visual clutter and enables the viewer to focus on the most crucial design elements.

Grids serve as foundational frameworks that guide the placement and alignment of elements in a layout. By providing consistency, order, and alignment, grid systems facilitate content organization and the creation of visually cohesive designs.

Typography refers to the selection, styling, and arrangement of type within a layout. It plays a crucial role in establishing the design's tone, mood, and personality, while also enhancing readability and conveying hierarchy.

Visual elements, including images, illustrations, icons, and graphics, are incorporated into a layout to complement and reinforce the message or information being conveyed. The selection of visual elements should be done thoughtfully to enhance the design's overall aesthetic appeal and effectiveness.

Responsive Design (for digital layouts) layouts must be able to adapt to various screen sizes and devices. Responsive design principles involve creating flexible layouts that gracefully adjust and reflow to accommodate different screen sizes and orientations while maintaining usability and visual coherence.

Overall, a well-executed layout is essential for creating visually compelling and effective designs that engage the audience, communicate information clearly, and achieve the intended design objectives.

10 Books that cover various aspects of design layout:

These books cover a range of topics related to layout design, including grid systems, composition principles, typography, and visual hierarchy. Whether you're a beginner learning the basics or an experienced designer refining your skills, these books offer valuable insights and resources for mastering layout design in graphic design.

"Grid Systems in Graphic Design" by Josef Müller-Brockmann - This classic book explores the principles and practical applications of grid systems in layout design.

"Layout Essentials: 100 Design Principles for Using Grids" by Beth Tondreau - This book offers practical advice and examples for using grids to create effective layouts in graphic design.

"Making and Breaking the Grid: A Graphic Design Layout Workshop" by Timothy Samara - This book provides an in-depth exploration of grid-based design principles and includes examples of layout designs from various designers.

"Layout Workbook: A Real-World Guide to Building Pages in Graphic Design" by Kristen Cullen - This workbook-style book offers practical exercises and examples to help designers master the fundamentals of layout design.

"Layout Design Types: Grids, Systems, and Design Systems" by Gavin Ambrose and Paul Harris - This book explores different types of layout design, including grids, systems, and design systems, with examples and case studies.

"Basics Design 02: Layout" by Gavin Ambrose and Paul Harris - This book provides an introduction to layout design principles and techniques, covering topics such as composition, hierarchy, and typography.

"The Non-Designer's Design Book" by Robin Williams - While not specifically focused on layout design, this book offers valuable insights into design principles, including layout, typography, and color, in an accessible and practical manner.

"Layout: The Design of the Printed Page" by Allen Hurlburt - This book delves into the principles and techniques of layout design for printed materials, covering topics such as page organization, typography, and visual hierarchy.

"Layout and Composition for Animation" by Ed Ghertner - While geared towards animation, this book covers layout and composition principles that are applicable to graphic design, including storytelling, staging, and visual rhythm.

"Layout: Workbook 2nd Edition" by Jim Krause - This workbook-style book offers practical exercises and examples to help designers improve their layout skills and develop their own unique style.

LAYOUT DESIGN TIPS FOR DESIGN BEGINNERS

Creating effective layouts is a crucial skill for graphic design beginners. A well-considered layout enhances visual appeal, guides the viewer's attention, and communicates information clearly.

Here are six tips to help beginning graphic designers improve their layouts:

1. Establish a Visual Hierarchy:

Design your layout with a clear visual hierarchy to guide the viewer's eyes through the content. Use variations in size, color, contrast, and placement to distinguish different elements. Make sure that important information stands out while maintaining a logical flow.

2. Use Grid Systems for Alignment:

Implement grid systems to establish a consistent and organized layout. Grids provide a framework for aligning elements, ensuring a structured composition. They help maintain visual balance and make it easier to organize content cohesively.

3. Strive for Balance and Symmetry:

Aim for balance in your layouts. Achieve balance through symmetrical or asymmetrical arrangements, depending on the design's requirements. Balancing visual weight helps create a harmonious and aesthetically pleasing composition.

4. Embrace Whitespace (Negative Space):

Embrace whitespace to prevent visual clutter and allow the design to breathe. Adequate negative space around elements enhances readability and prevents the viewer from feeling overwhelmed. Whitespace can also highlight key elements and contribute to an elegant design.

5. Maintain Consistent Alignment and Margins:

Keep alignment and margins consistent throughout the layout. Whether using left, right, center, or justified alignment, strive for uniformity to achieve a polished look. Consistent margins contribute to a sense of order and professionalism.

6. Practice Makes Perfect:

There's no such thing as a perfect layout. Be motivated to design a layout that works, meaning a layout in which the message effectively reaches the target audience by adhering to the elements and principles of design, while also being creative with your text and images. Graphic design involves much more than just making things look pretty and perfect or settling for what appeals to you. This means that you should create multiple layouts, not just "The One."

BONUS TIP:
Align elements with imaginary lines

Use invisible lines to align and organize elements. Aligning text, images, and other elements along horizontal or vertical lines creates a sense of order and cohesion. This technique aids in creating a visually pleasing and well-structured layout.

The effectiveness of a layout depends on the context and the intended audience. Experiment with different layouts, seek feedback, and refine your designs based on the principles of visual hierarchy, balance, and consistency. As you gain experience, you'll develop an intuitive sense of what works best for different projects and design scenarios.

Strive for each layout to have a focal point that can captures the viewer's attention, whether it's a headline, an image, or even just color. Sometimes one isolated element captures one's attention.

Purposeful Layouts

The first impression in any layout is vital, followed by a purposeful second look, as you cannot control how the third or fourth will be perceived. Understanding your audience is crucial; know what they have appreciated before so you can design a layout that engages them again.

Engage in Design Thinking and The Process

Design thinking is crucial in the layout and the design process as it promotes a human-centric approach, emphasizing empathy, brainstorming, and refinement. By empathizing with the end user, designers gain insights to create layouts that address specific needs and preferences. This methodology guarantees that designs are not just visually appealing but also functionally effective, enhancing user engagement and satisfaction. Design thinking, with its focus on comprehending and solving actual user problems, enhances the overall quality and impact of layouts in the design process.

Remember the aim is to create a layout where the message effectively reaches the target audience by following the elements and principles of design. Be creative with your text and images. Your layout should include a focal point that grabs the reader's attention, whether it's a headline, an image, or a color.

The Design/Client Brief

A design/client brief serves as a foundation for any design project and outlines the expectations, requirements, goals, and preferences. The purpose of a design brief is to ensure that the designer understands the client's vision and can create a solution that meets the client's needs. It is common for designers to create their own briefs from a client meeting. While clients may provide initial information and objectives for a project, designers often take detailed notes during the meeting to ensure they fully understand the client's needs, expectations, and vision. They then create a design brief based on the meeting to serve as a comprehensive guide for the project. A well-crafted design/client brief is crucial for a successful and effective design project.

A typical design brief may include the following components:

Project Overview: A brief description of the project, its goals, and its intended audience, along with clear objectives and specific goals that the client wants to achieve through the design.

Target Audience: Information about the intended audience or users for the design, including demographics, preferences, and behaviors.

Scope of Work: Clearly defined boundaries and limitations of the project, including specific deliverables and any constraints.

Brand Guidelines: If applicable, information about the client's brand, including logos, colors, and other visual elements that should be incorporated into the design.

Budget and Timeline: Any budgetary constraints and deadlines for the project.

Competitor Information: Insight into competitors or similar projects that the client likes or dislikes, helping the designer understand the client's preferences.

Functional Requirements: Specific features or functionalities that the design should incorporate.

Aesthetic Preferences: Visual style preferences, including examples of designs or styles that the client finds appealing or unappealing.

Communication and Approval Process: Details about how the client and designer will communicate, provide feedback, and approve design concepts throughout the project.

Remember that having a well-defined design brief is crucial for the success of a project as it helps align the expectations of both the client and the designer(s), ensuring that the final deliverables meet the client's needs and vision. With a clear understanding of the client's needs, designers can work more efficiently, saving time and resources. For this reason the importance of teamwork cannot be overstated.

The Re Spa & Gym Branding (based on a design brief)

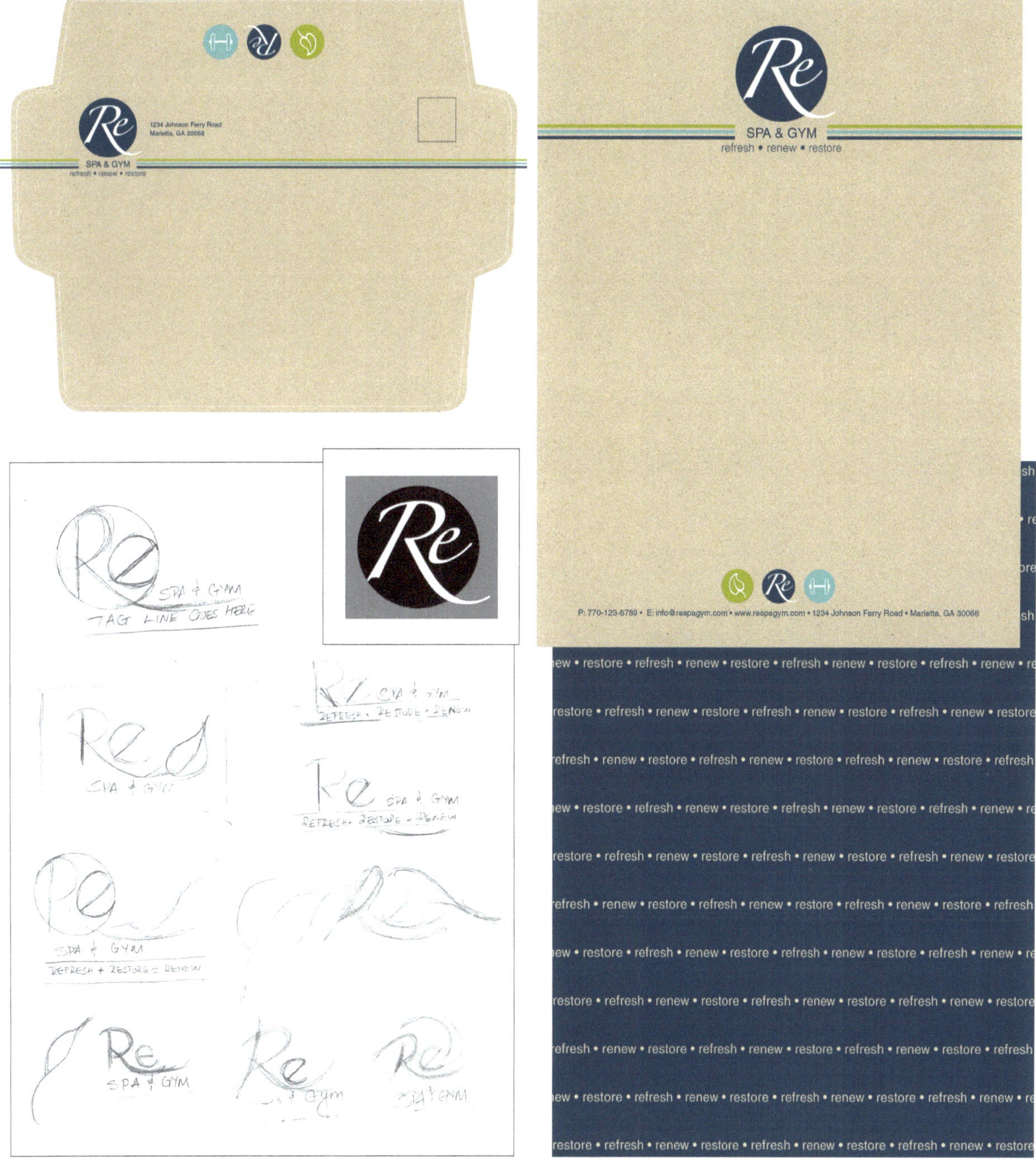

These thumbnails represent the first steps in the logo ideation process and display the chosen developed logo, which was approved by the client (positioned at the top right inset). The company's slogan, "refresh • restore • renew," was later incorporated. Once the brand identity (logo) received final approval, a master letterhead and envelope were created for three color-coded areas of the **Re Spa & Gym** branding. To enhance uniqueness and brand recognition, the slogan "renew • restore • refresh" is featured on the back of the letterhead. The logo was subsequently applied to various brand touchpoints, as showcased on the following spread.

Student Design Team: Brieanna Bailey and Lucy Kimundi / Kennesaw State University.

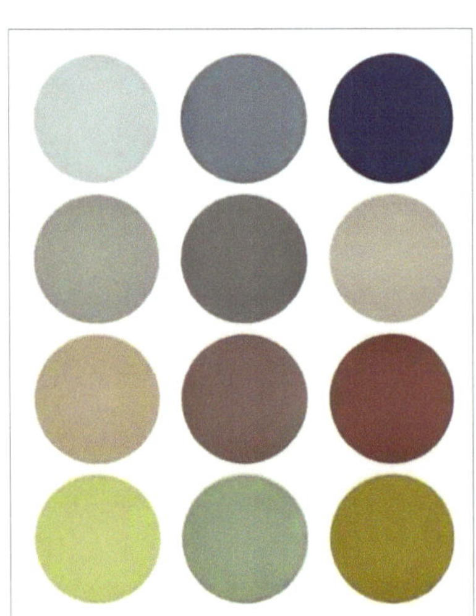

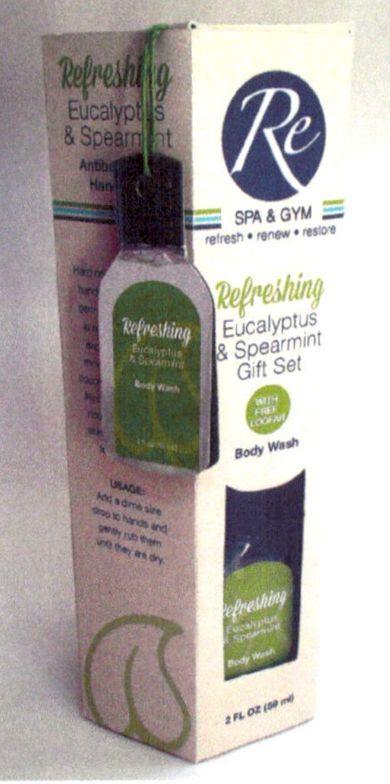

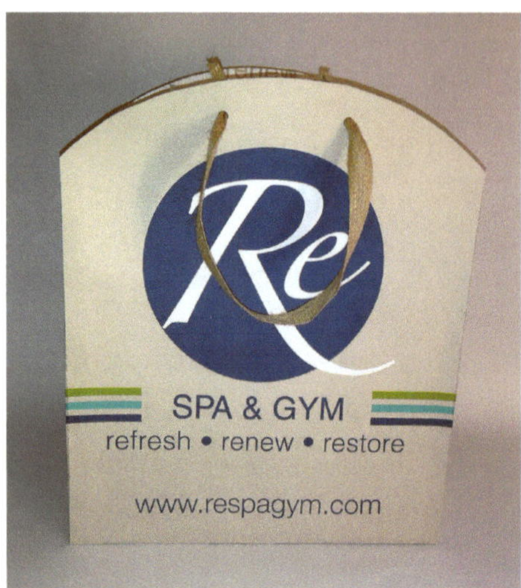

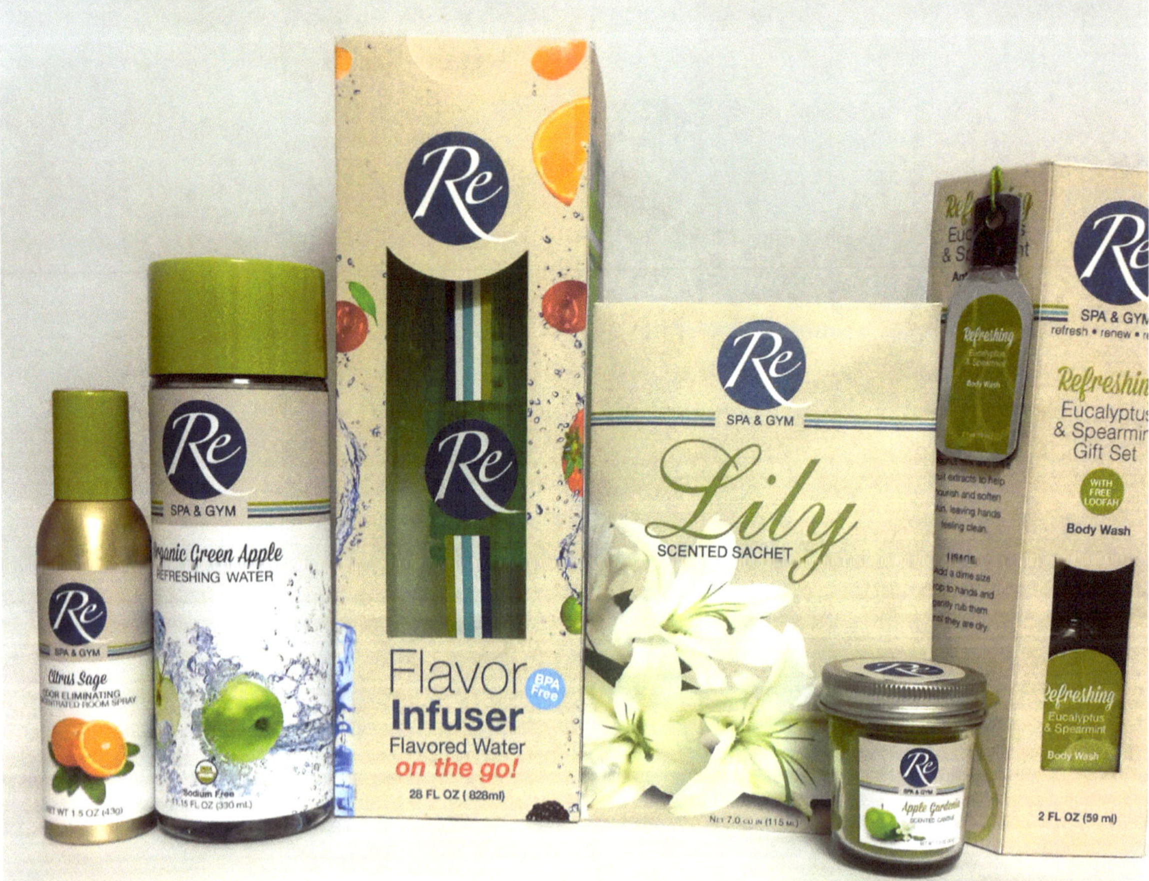

Based on the design brief, the student design team worked diligently to establish brand recognition and a cohesive visual identity for the Re Spa & Gym brand. They used different strategies to ensure consistency and unity in the visual presentation of products. This included a dedicated color palette, typography, imagery, style, and other relevant design elements. The team created mockups for various items such as bags, boxes, packets, labels, and die-cuts, all of which maintained consistency across the brand. This was crucial in building a strong and recognizable brand.

Student Design Team: *Brieanna Bailey and Lucy Kimundi / Kennesaw State University.*

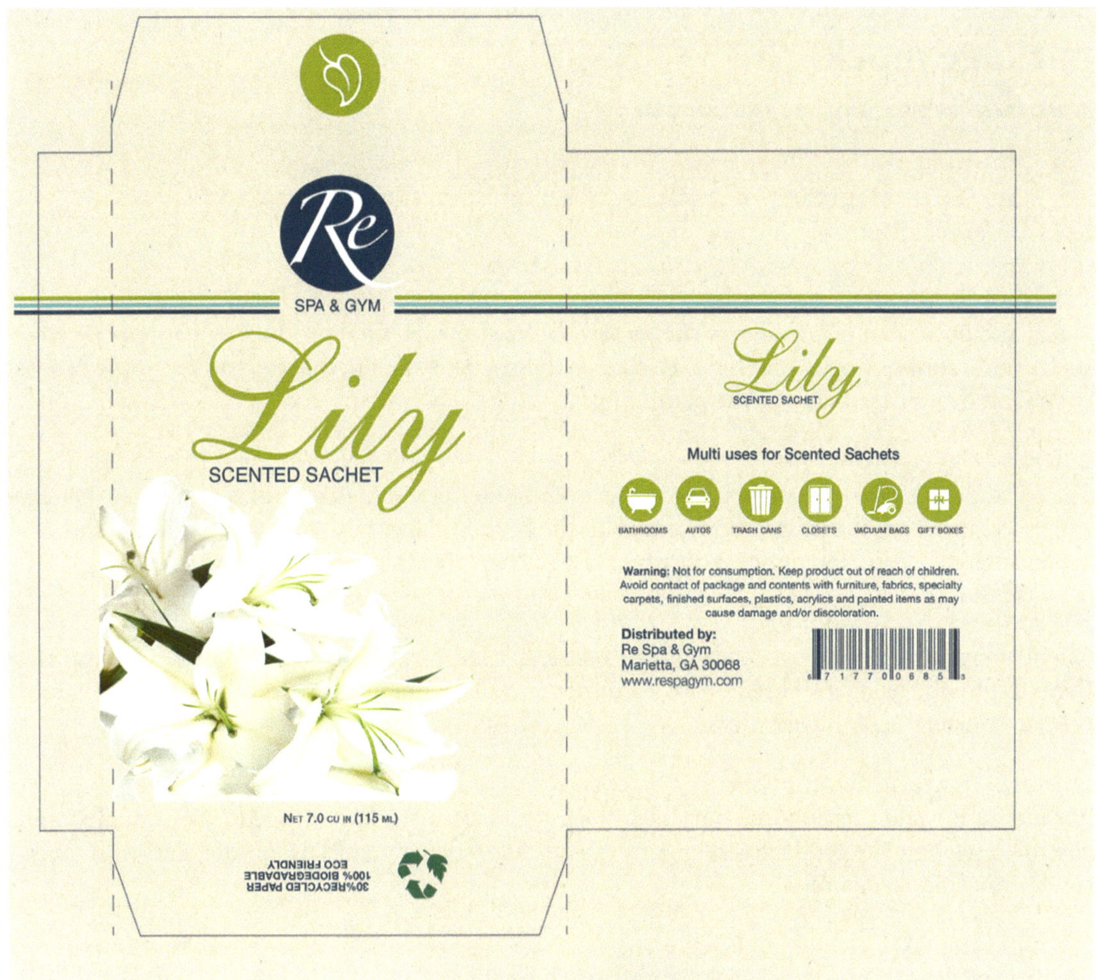

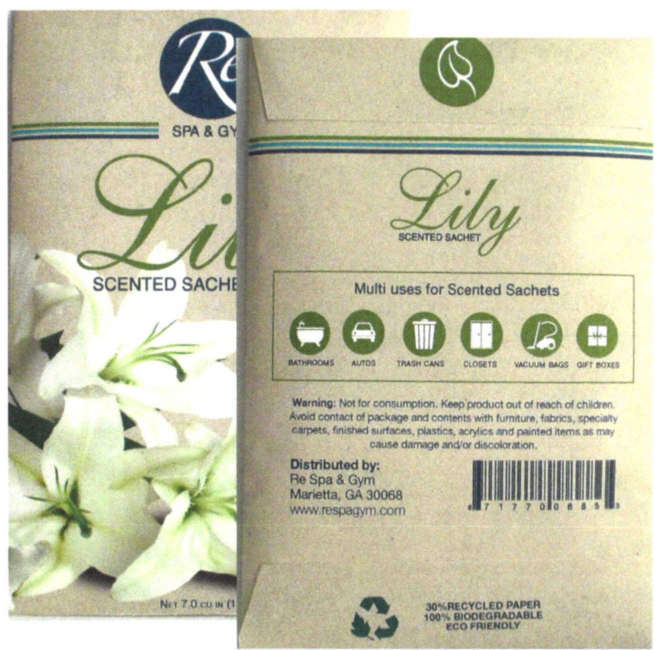

Based on the design brief, several mockups were developed for different scented sachet packets as part of the design process. Thorough research was conducted to ensure adherence to a correct list of restrictions and safety information.

The importance of realistic and compelling package mockups

The importance of a package mockup resembling the actual product for client feedback lies in its ability to provide a realistic representation of the final product. This is crucial for several reasons:

1. Visual Realism:
A realistic package mockup allows clients to visualize how the final product will appear on store shelves or in promotional materials. This helps them make informed decisions about the design, color, and overall aesthetics of the packaging.

2. Brand Perception:
The packaging is often a significant part of a brand's identity. A lifelike mockup ensures that clients can assess how well the packaging aligns with the brand image they want to convey. It allows for a more accurate evaluation of how consumers might perceive the product on the market.

3. Feedback Accuracy:
Clients may have specific expectations or preferences for the packaging. A realistic mockup enables them to provide feedback based on an accurate representation of the final product, leading to more precise and actionable suggestions.

4. Marketing and Promotion:
For marketing and promotional purposes, having a realistic package mockup is essential. It allows clients to see how the product will look in various advertising materials, online platforms, and other promotional channels.

5. Consumer Appeal:
Realistic packaging mockups help clients gauge how the product will stand out on the shelf and attract consumers. Elements like color, typography, and imagery can significantly impact consumer appeal, and a true-to-life mockup ensures that these elements are accurately represented.

6. Cost Savings:
Creating accurate mockups early in the design process can help prevent costly revisions later on. It allows clients to address potential issues or make necessary changes before production begins, reducing the risk of expensive modifications after the packaging is in print.

7. Client Confidence:
A lifelike package mockup instills confidence in clients by demonstrating that the design team understands their vision and can deliver a product that meets their expectations. This can lead to smoother project workflows and more satisfied clients.

In summary, a package mockup that closely resembles the final product is essential for effective client feedback because it provides a tangible and accurate representation. This helps clients make informed decisions about the packaging design, leading to successful product launches and marketing campaigns.

The Design Brief: Design new and creative packaging for any product purchased from a vending machine and an accompanying poster-size creative ad. The ad is to be placed next to the vending machine or in the student campus newspaper. Do not use the actual packaged product as the main image in the ad. Show your template research for the package. Create the production flat for the final package and construct a well-crafted realistic looking 3-D mockup for presentation.

Remember to follow the design brief and engage in package template research or construct your own creative package.

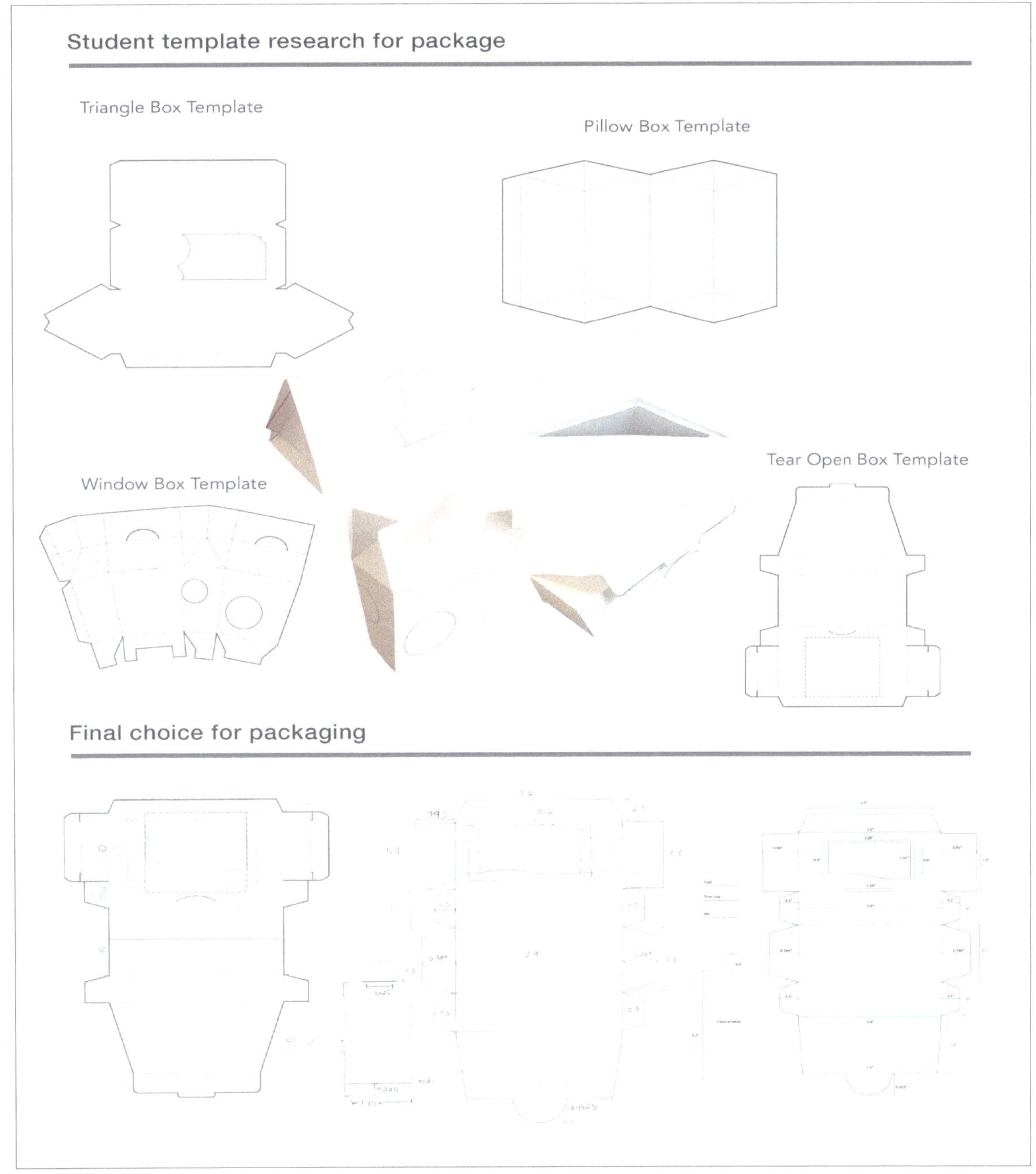

Final template thumbnails from the designer's research and mini mockups of each template are shown, as well as the final choice of the "Tear Open Box Template" for the 3-D mockups of the new vending machine Fruit Snacks package.

Student Designer: *Lucy Kimundi / Kennesaw State University.*

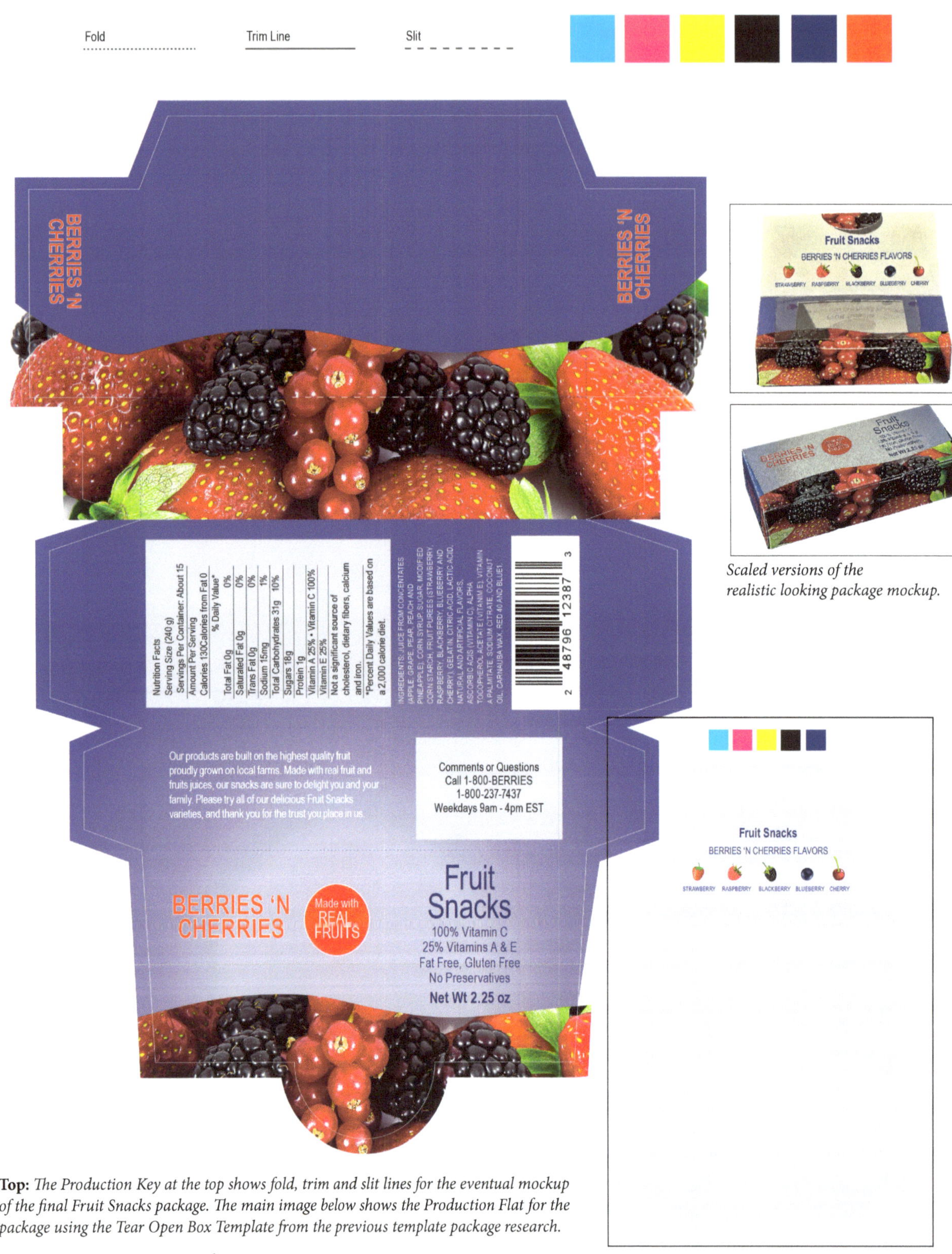

Scaled versions of the realistic looking package mockup.

Top: *The Production Key at the top shows fold, trim and slit lines for the eventual mockup of the final Fruit Snacks package. The main image below shows the Production Flat for the package using the Tear Open Box Template from the previous template package research.*

Student Designer: *Lucy Kimundi / Kennesaw State University.*

The inside of the Production Flat (scaled).

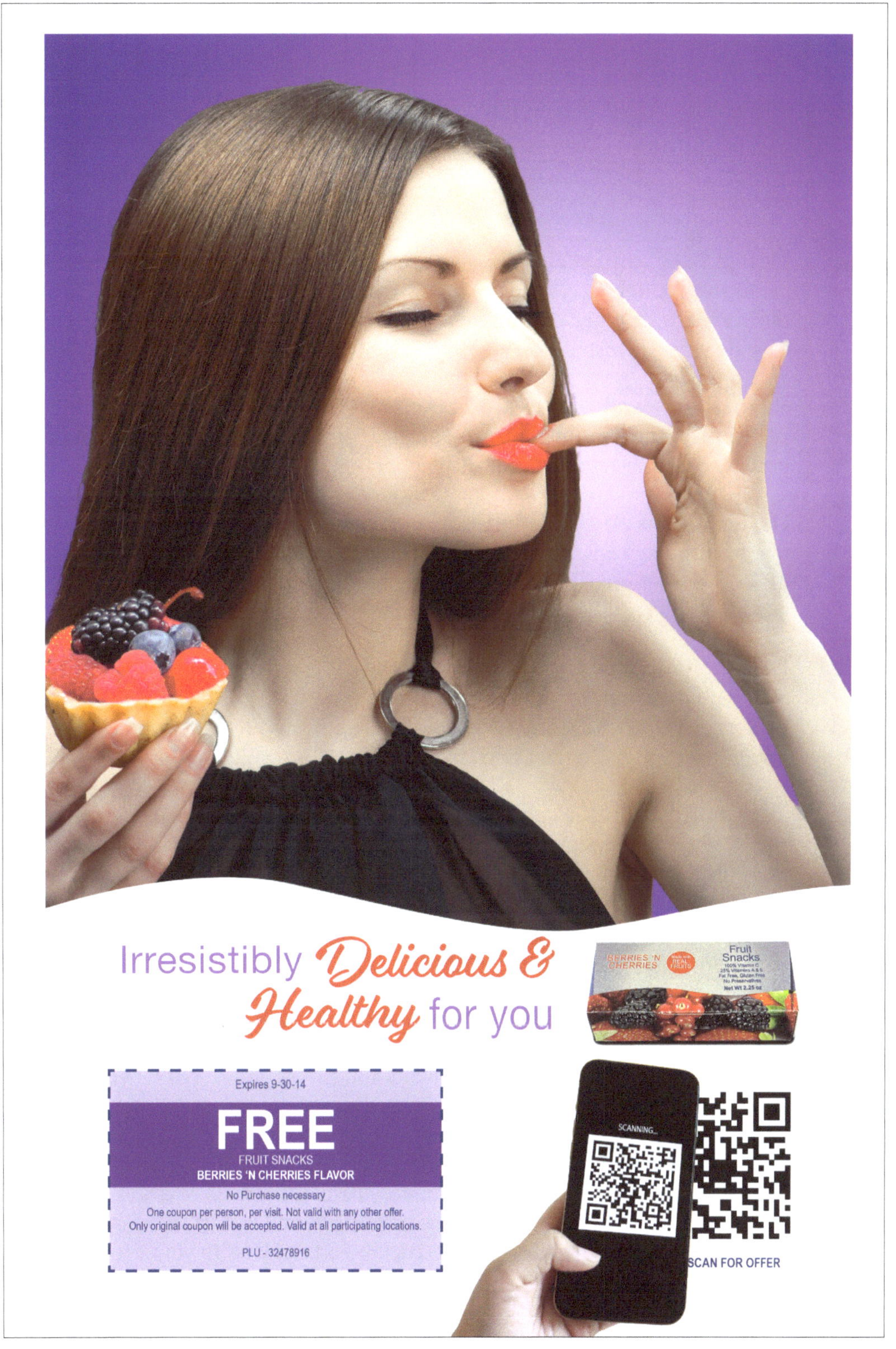

Full page/poster size creative ad for the launch of the new Fruit Snacks product with time sensitive coupon. Clever use of the QR scanner to access more details of the product.

Student Designer: *Lucy Kimundi / Kennesaw State University.*

FINDING INSPIRATION FOR CREATING COMPELLING DESIGN MOCKUPS

You should now be ready to begin the creation of a portfolio of well-crafted mockups for effectively showcasing your skills. A well-designed portfolio acts as a visual resume, enabling potential clients or employers to evaluate your design style, creativity, and technical expertise.

Here are some suggestions for various sources you can explore to find inspiration for your design mockups.

Design Blogs and Websites: Check out design-focused blogs, websites, and online platforms like Behance, Dribbble, Awwwards, and Designspiration. These platforms showcase a wide range of design projects, including mockups, branding, and more. They provide valuable inspiration and insights into current design trends and best practices.

Retail Stores and Supermarkets: Visit local stores and supermarkets to observe current packaging trends in your industry. Pay attention to how different products are presented on shelves and at the display shelves at the end of aisles.

Design Books and Magazines: Explore design books, magazines, and publications that feature mockups, design case studies, and visual inspiration. Books on graphic design, web design, UI/UX design, and branding often include examples of design mockups and provide valuable insights into the design process and creative concepts.

Design Templates and Resources: Browse design marketplaces and websites that offer templates, mockup kits, and design resources for purchase or free download. Platforms like Adobe Stock, Creative Market, Envato Elements, and GraphicRiver offer a wide selection of design assets, including mockup templates for various design projects.

Real-world Examples and Observations: Draw inspiration from the world around you by observing design elements in everyday life, such as signage, packaging, advertisements, and product displays. Pay attention to typography, layout, color schemes, and visual hierarchy in physical and digital environments, and consider how these elements can be applied to your design mockups.

University Students Showcase: Reviewing the work of design students from recognized universities and student competitions such as GDUSA, Society of Publication Designers, The One Show, and others can be helpful. Explore students' digital portfolios, to find design elements and presentation styles. University students also use image banks for some of their creative solutions.

Nature and Art: Seek inspiration from nature, art, architecture, and other creative disciplines beyond graphic design. Explore natural patterns, textures, colors, and shapes, as well as artistic movements, cultural influences, and historical references that can inform your design mockups and add depth and richness to your creative concepts.

Personal Experiences and Experimentation: Draw inspiration from your own experiences, and interests to infuse personal elements into your design mockups. Allow yourself to experiment and explore new ideas, techniques, and approaches when creating design mockups. Don't be afraid to push boundaries, try out unconventional concepts, and take creative risks to discover new possibilities and unlock your creative potential.

STUDENTS SHOWCASE OF
CREATIVE DESIGN MOCKUPS

The Design Brief: Create a new brand of home interior paints and a line of products that evoke the style of a recognized graphic designer while still appealing to a specified audience. Reflect the spirit of the designer. Begin with the research for your chosen designer before cresting the brand's identity (logo) wich will first be applied to the business card, letterhead, and envelope.

Vivid's brand's identity was applied to other touchpoints of the brand, as seen on the next spread.

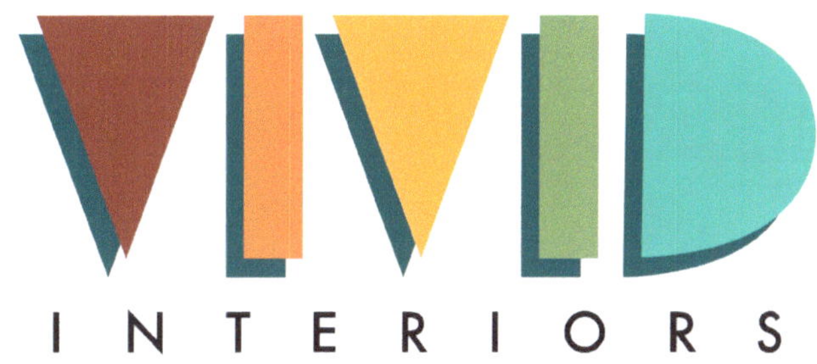

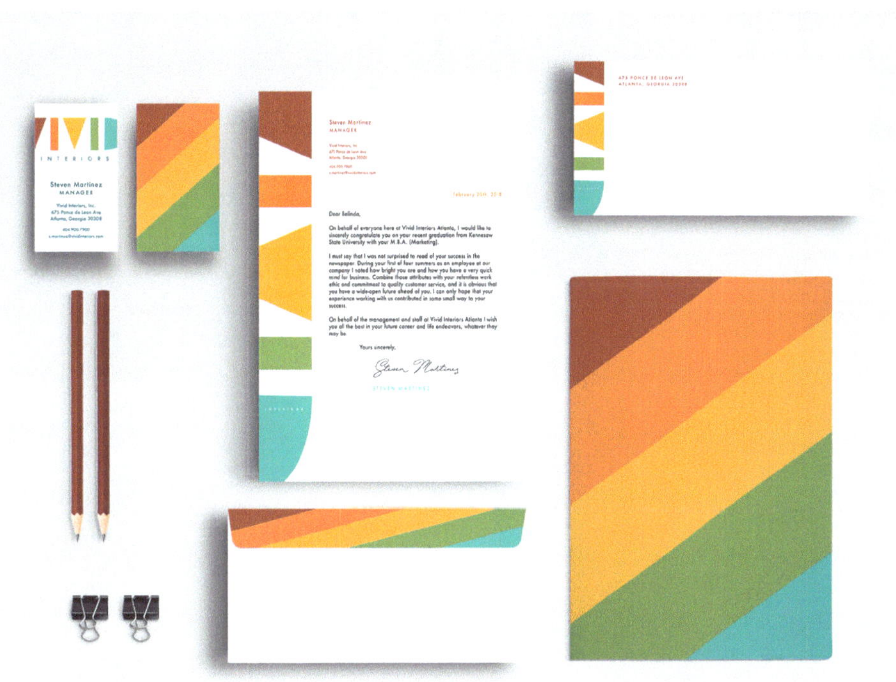

After studying the brief, this student team chose Aaron James Draplin, an American graphic designer, entrepreneur and author based in Portland, Oregon. After brainstorming, each student on the team was assigned to work on a specific area of the bold and colorful product line for the new brand of interior paints called VIVID, which consisted of all things paint, from different size paint cans, labels, sleeves for brushes and rollers, aprons, etc. This presentation of the brand's identity and system consisted of a cohesive stationery set designed by one student.

Student Designer: *Rachel Fred / Kennesaw State University.*

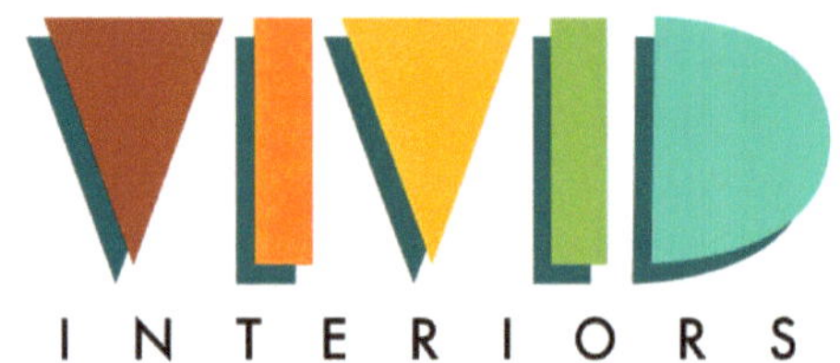

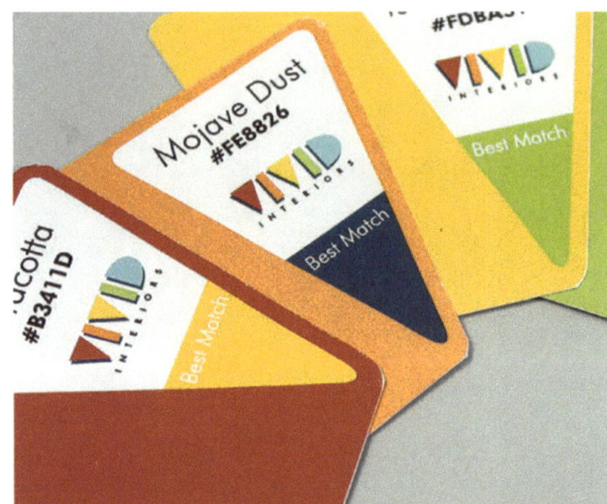

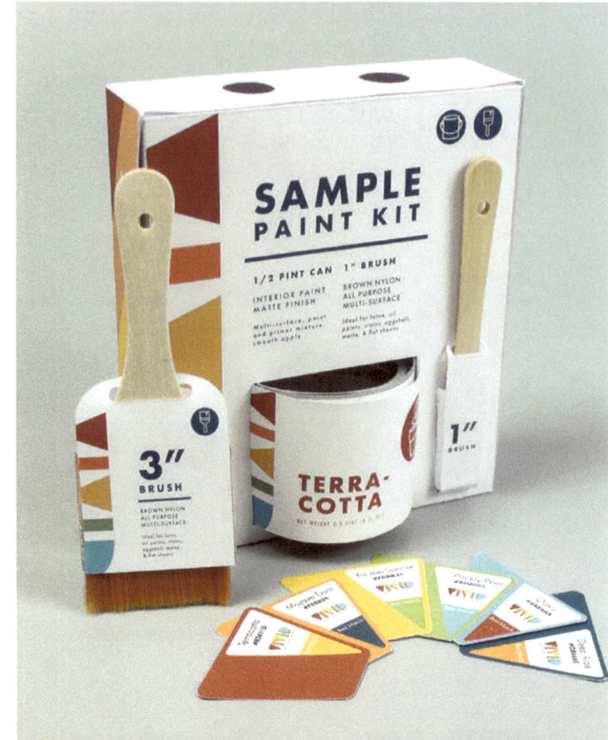

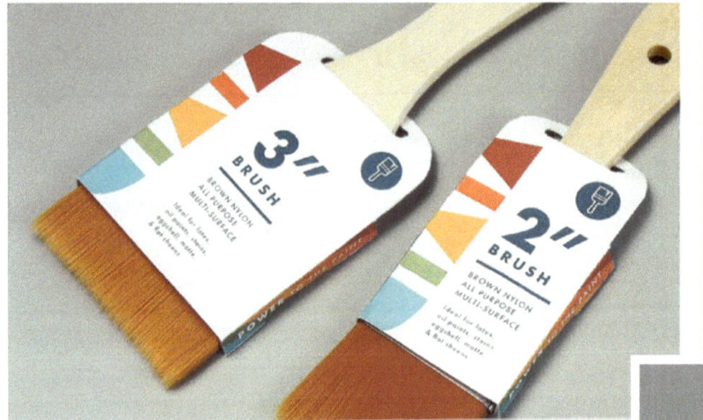

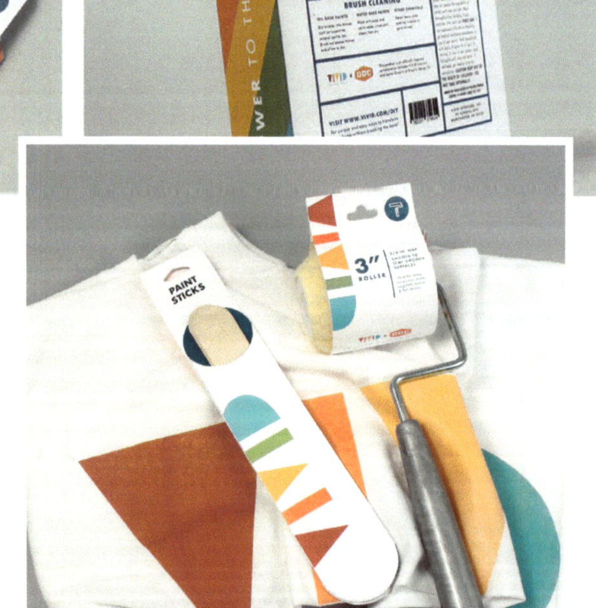

VIVID'S colorful and visually cohesive brand itentity as applied to all things paint: paint color chips, sample paint kit, brushes, rollers and paint sticks.

Student Design Team: Rachel Fred, Payton Butler, Justin Hilton, Audrey Lockstedt / *Kennesaw State University.*

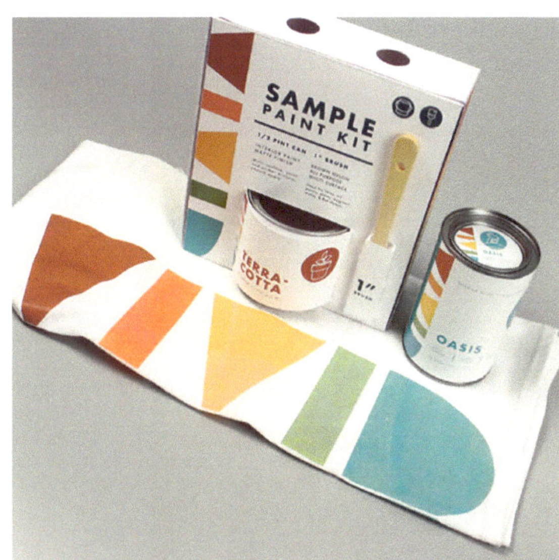

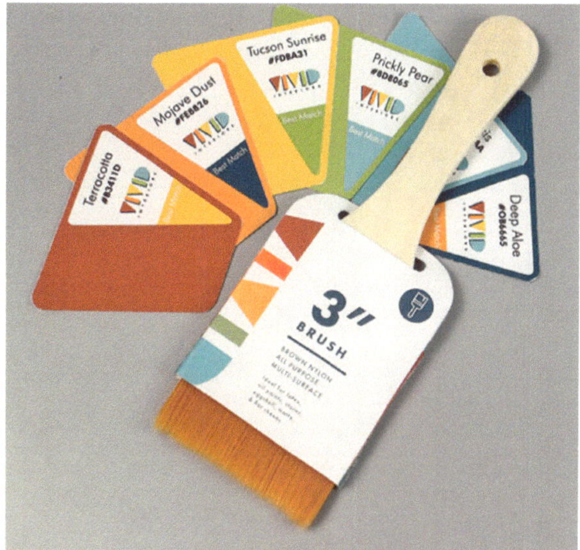

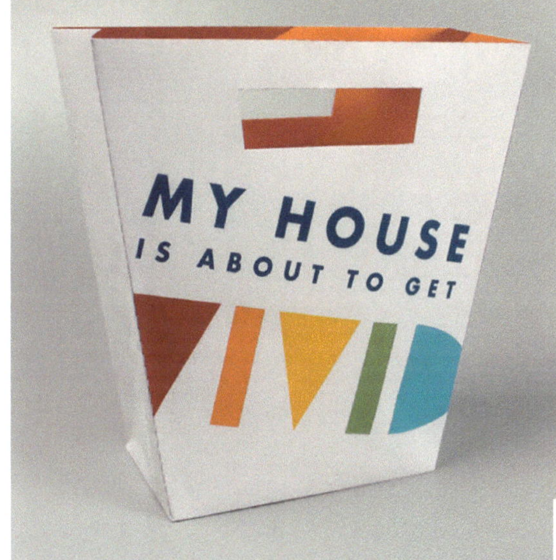

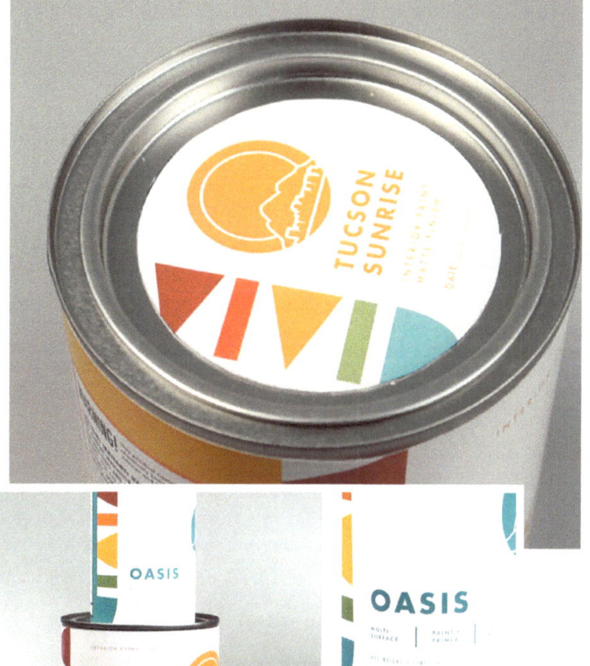

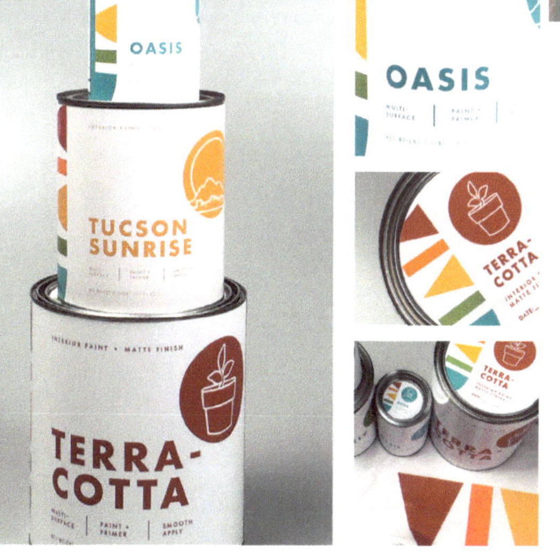

*The application of VIVID'S colorful and bold brand itentity
as applied to different sized paint cans, drop cloths, color chips,
small sturdy bags designed to hold small items, etc.*

The Design Brief: Design a 16-page booklet for a consumer product. The booklet must be available where the product is sold. Conceptualize a creative location map for the booklet's back cover.

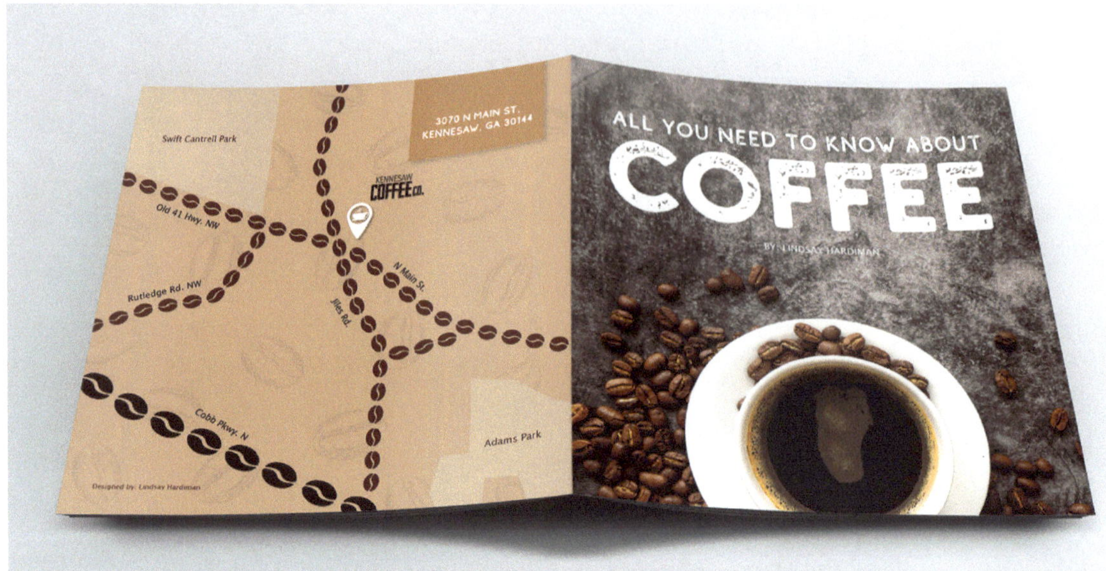

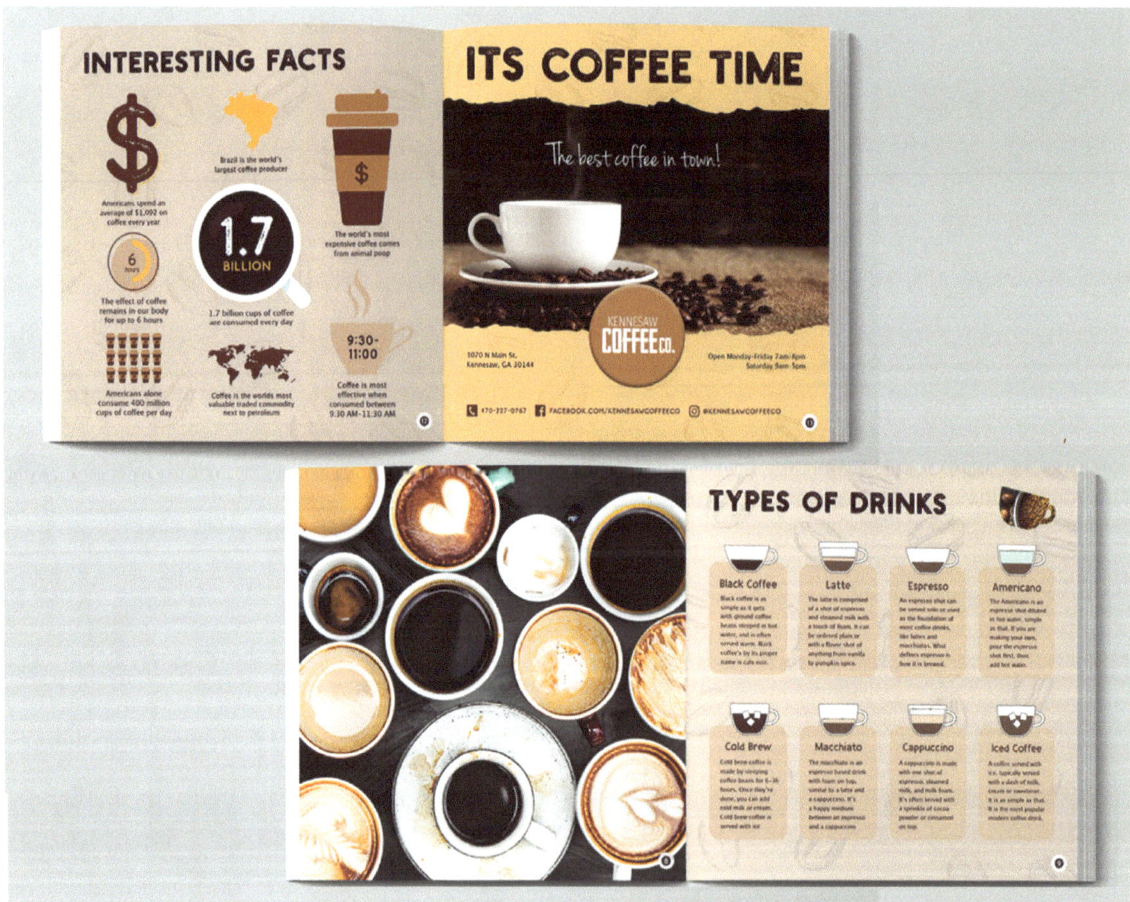

Cover and page spreads from the 16-page booklet on "All You Need to Know About Coffee." Spreads shows good alignment, spatial relationships, a thoughtful color palette and overall visual cohesiveness.

Student Designer: *Lindsay Muncy / Kennesaw State University.*

The Design Brief: Design branding for a restaurant of your choice. Brand touchpoints: menu, 16-page Annual Report, Special Occasion Recipe Book (design one recipe spread for presentation).

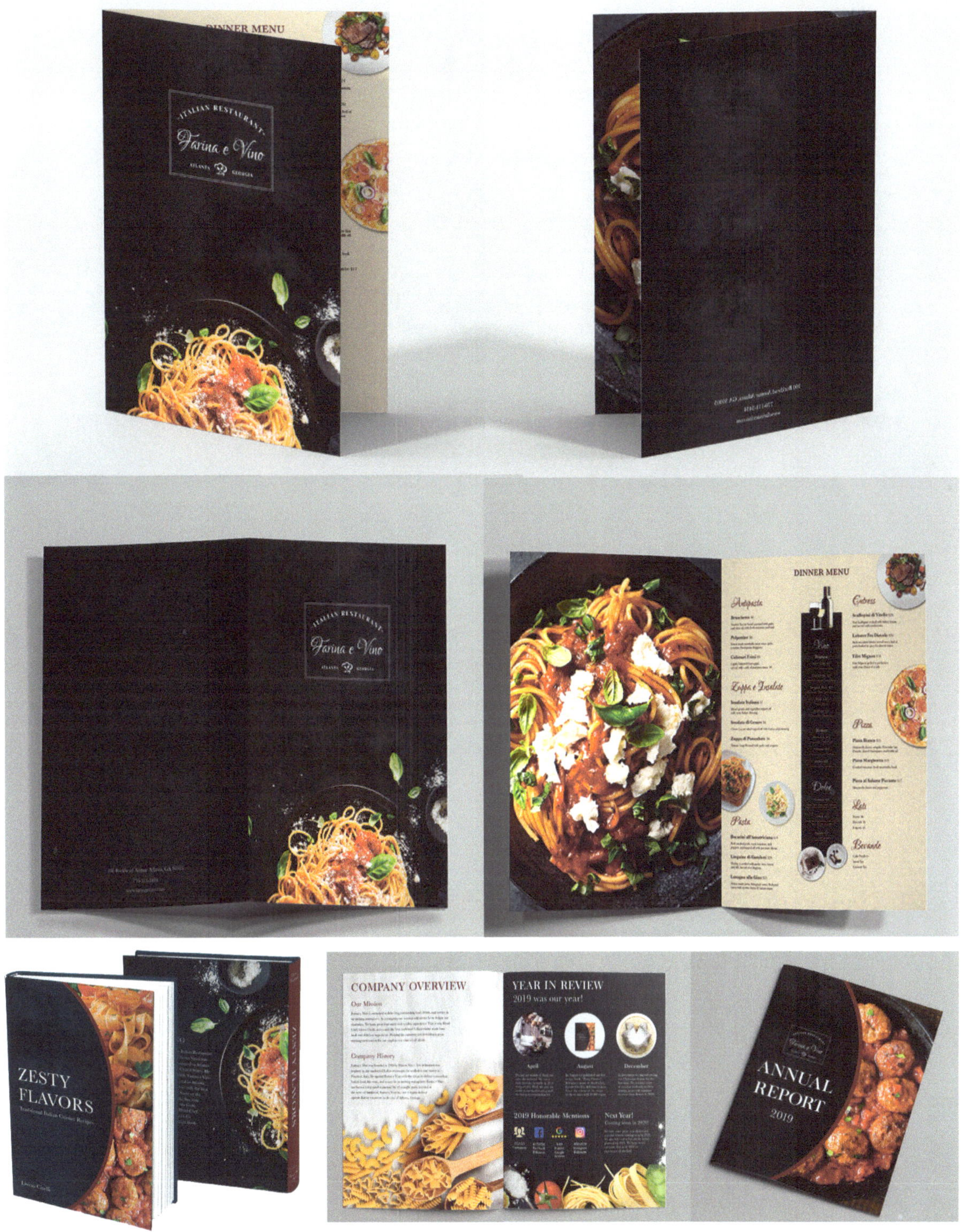

Student mockups for an upscale Italian restaurant. Items include: menu, annual report and recipe book w/recipe spread.

Student Designer: *Lindsay Muncy / Kennesaw State University.*

The Design Brief: Design a 16-page Annual Report for a restaurant of your choice. Research the content for the cover and inner pages of the annual report. Create headlines for each section and placeholder text for the body copy.

The entire publication should have a visually cohesive design, with sections covering the company's overview, the year in review, plans for the future, and other highlights and activities of the company. Create a color palette based on the images you plan to use. This will involve researching and locating high-resolution images. The color scheme should align with the restaurant's branding.

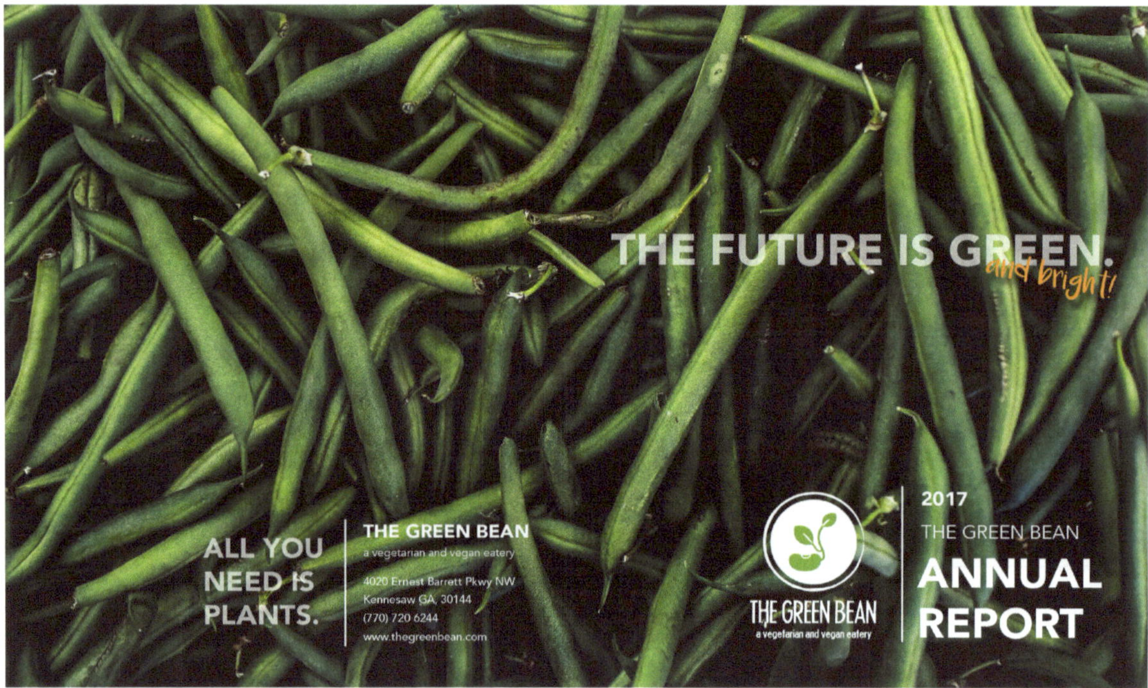

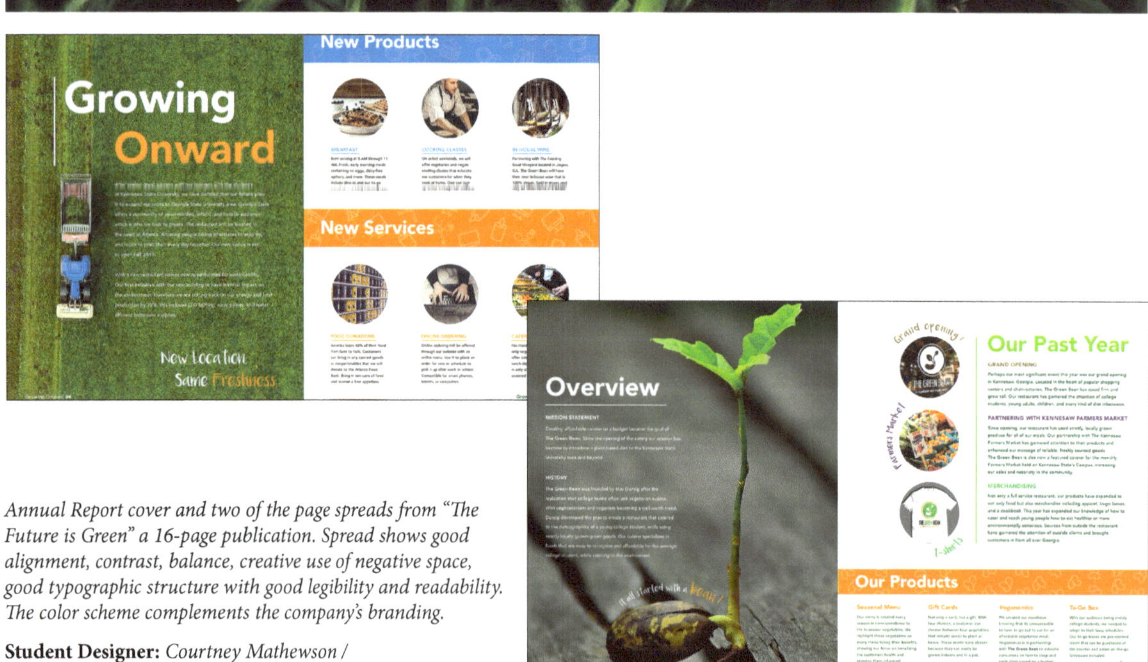

Annual Report cover and two of the page spreads from "The Future is Green" a 16-page publication. Spread shows good alignment, contrast, balance, creative use of negative space, good typographic structure with good legibility and readability. The color scheme complements the company's branding.

Student Designer: *Courtney Mathewson /*
Kennesaw State University.

The Design Brief: Design a 16-page Annual Report for a restaurant of your choice. Research the content for the cover and inner pages of the annual report. Create headlines for each section and placeholder text for the body copy.

The entire publication should have a visually cohesive design, with sections covering the company's overview, the year in review, plans for the future, and other highlights and activities of the company. Create a color palette based on the images you plan to use. This will involve researching and locating high-resolution images. The color scheme should align with the restaurant's branding.

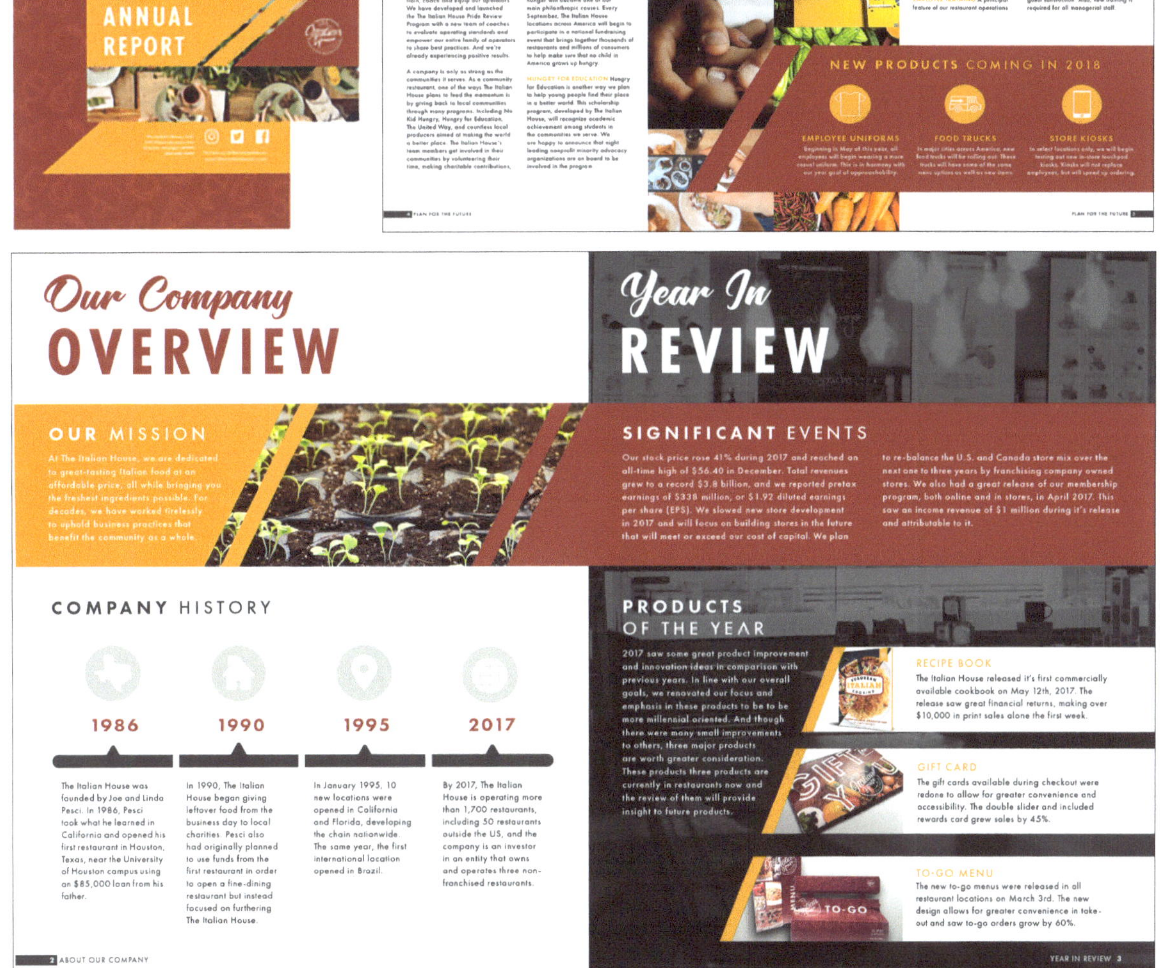

Top left image shows a thumbnail view of the annual report's cover. Inner spreads show good alignment, contrast, balance, creativity, thoughtful use of negative space, and well-structured typographic hierarchy showing good legibility and readability. The color scheme complements company's branding.

Student Designer: *Rachel Fred / Kennesaw State University.*

The Design Brief: Conceptualize new and creative packaging for ONE inexpensive delicate, light fabric item such as men's ties, scarves, underwear, headwraps, etc., accompanied by a creative ad for the product. The packaging must make the product appear to be more expensive. The ad is to be placed in a consumer publication of the target audience.

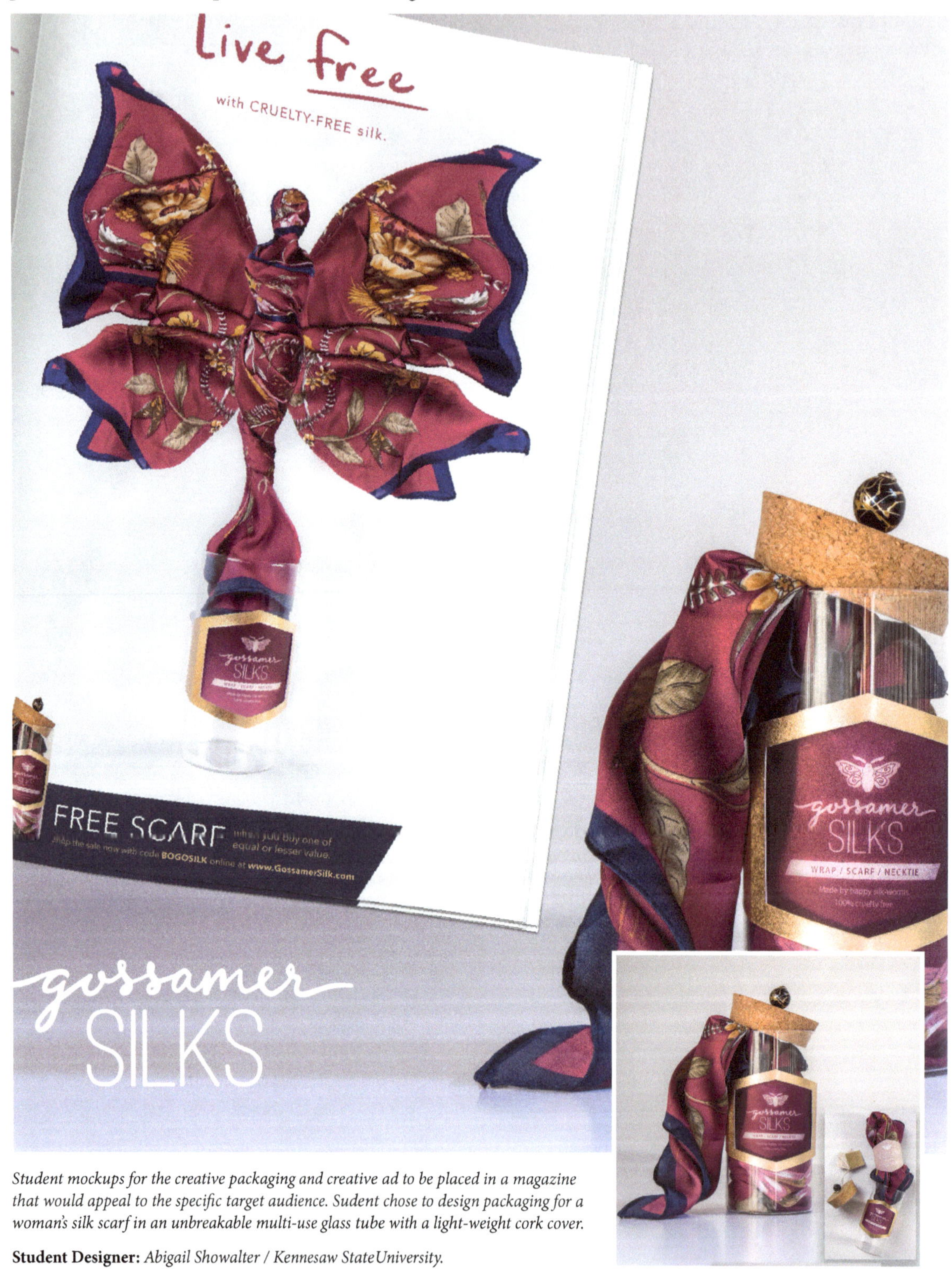

Student mockups for the creative packaging and creative ad to be placed in a magazine that would appeal to the specific target audience. Sudent chose to design packaging for a woman's silk scarf in an unbreakable multi-use glass tube with a light-weight cork cover.

Student Designer: *Abigail Showalter / Kennesaw State University.*

The Design Brief: Conceptualize new and creative packaging for ONE inexpensive delicate, light-weight fabric item such as men's ties, scarves, tube top, leggings, underwear, headwraps, etc., accompanied by a creative ad for the product. The packaging must make the product appear to be more expensive. The ad is to be placed in a consumer publication of the target audience.

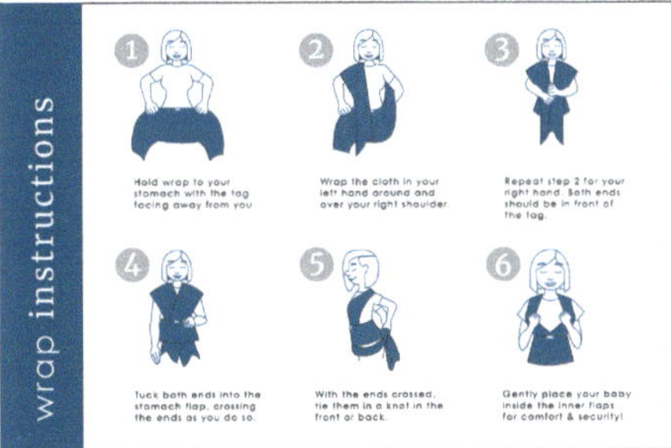

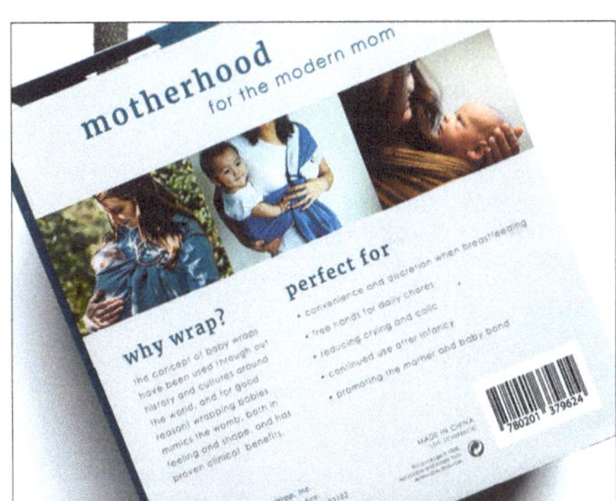

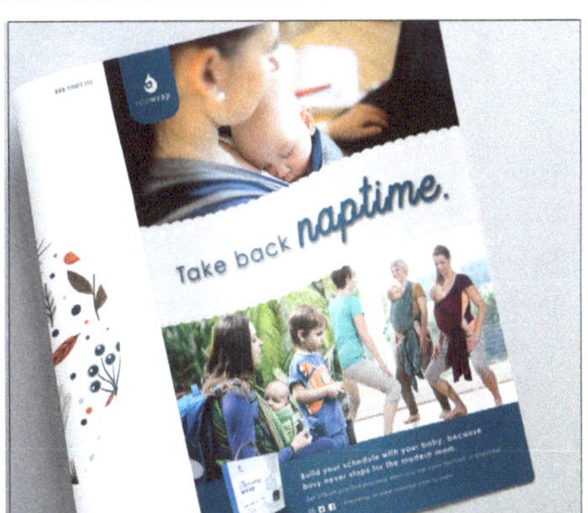

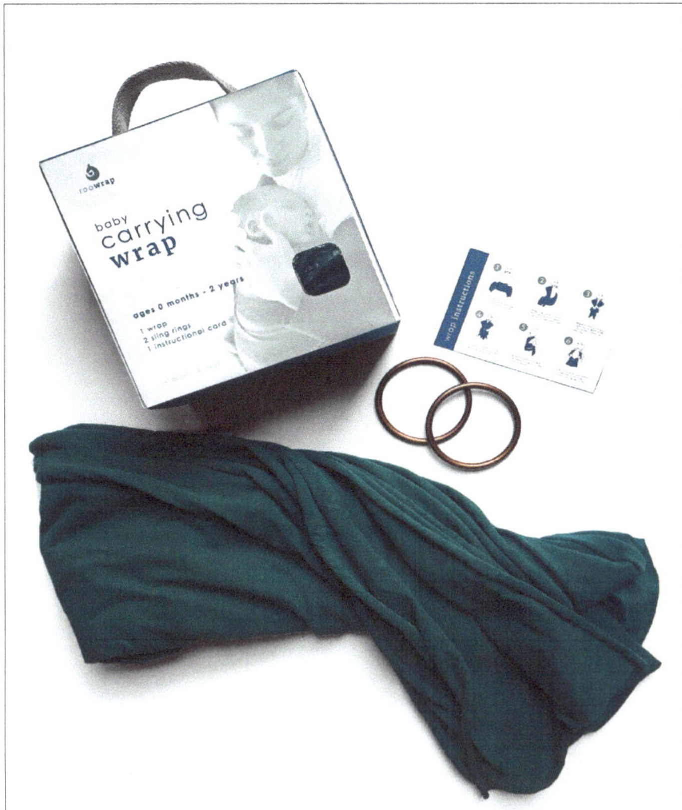

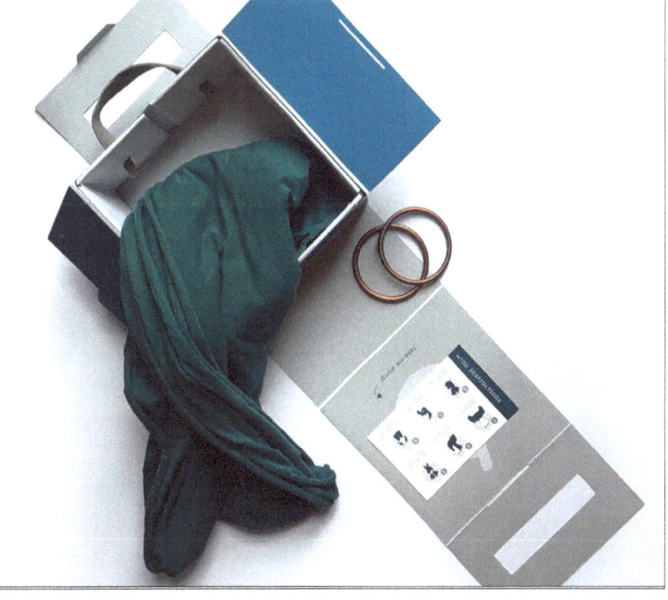

Student mockups for the Roo Wrap project. Student designed packaging for a baby-carrying wrap, with complete instructions on its use. Student design of the logo, ad sturdy box packaging with an accompanying creative ad placed in a consumer magazine of the target audience. Stock images were purchased and used for the ad.

Student Designer: *Rachel Fred / Kennesaw State University.*

The Design Brief: Design and mockup a six pack set of 2-inch cubes containing household or personal items of your choice. Package the six cubes so they fit well in one larger container. Research and place all design and brand elements as required on the inner and outer packaging. All packages must be hand crafted with sturdy materials suitable for mailing. Take several photographic views for placement into your portfolio.

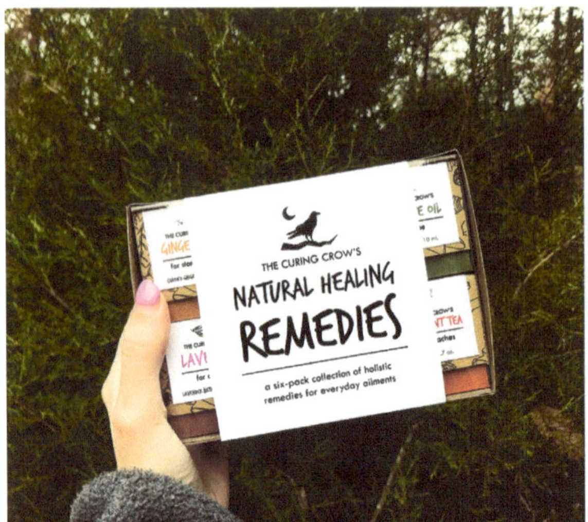
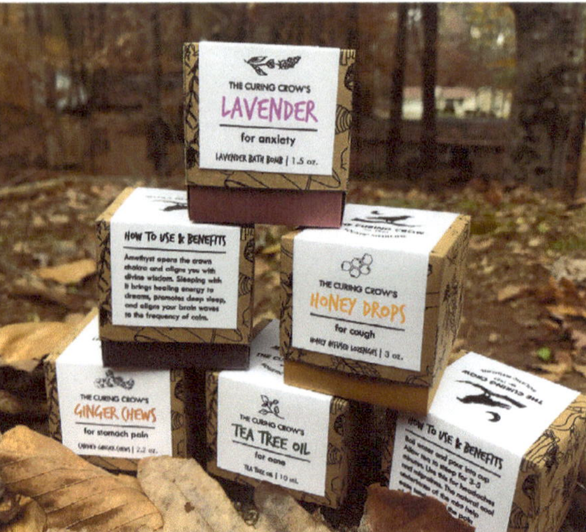
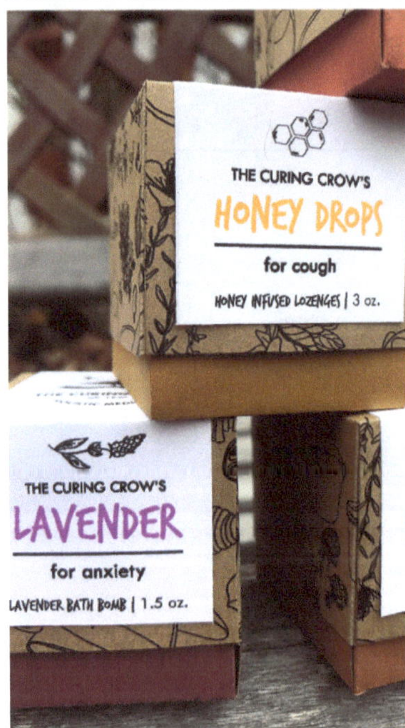
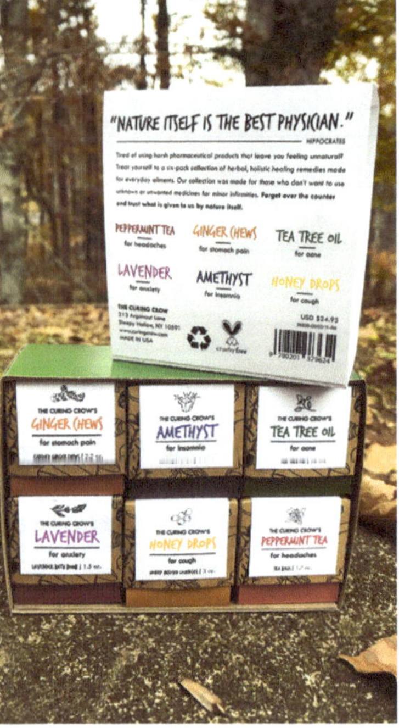
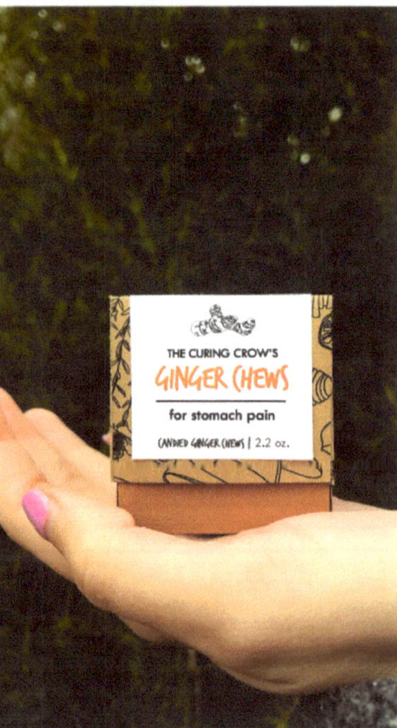

Student's final design mockups for the 2-inch square cubes, each cube holding an item from the set, for the product, The Curing Crow Natural Healing Remedies. All six cubes were eventaully packaged in one outer package snugly holding them all. All design and brand elements were placed as required on the inner and outer packaging. Student physically created all mockups for all packaging. No ready-made containers were used. Student took creative photographs of the completed project for showcasing in their portfolio.

Student Designer: *Courtney Mathewson / Kennesaw State University.*

The Design Brief: Design one 2-inch cube package for a household or personal product of your choice. Consider all sides of the package, including the inner area, paying attention to color, typography, and image cohesiveness. Research and place all design and brand elements as required on the packaging. Take photographic views for presentation. Create the production flat and an ad for the product to be placed in an appropriate consumer magazine.

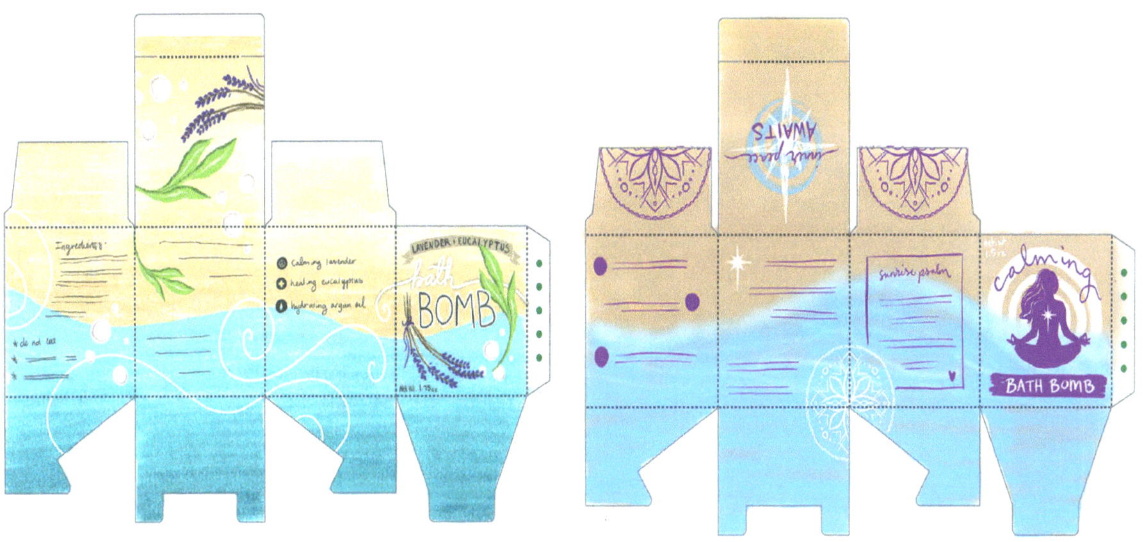

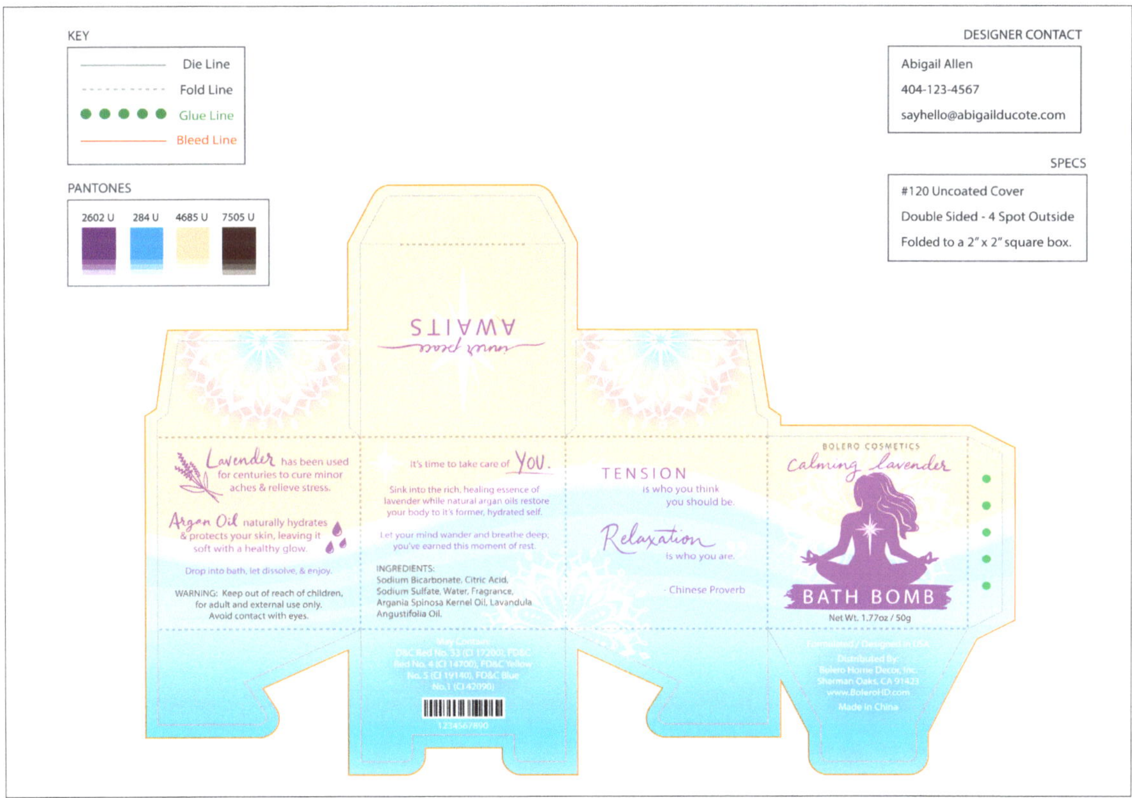

Above: *Student's creative ideation for cube package showing cdifferent possible color solutions for one bath bomb, typography placement and other design elements. Ideation done on a digital tablet.*

Below: *Production Flat with Key and other production details to assist with the construction of mockups. (Mockups and ad on following spread).*

Student Designer: *Abigail Showalter / Kennesaw State University.*

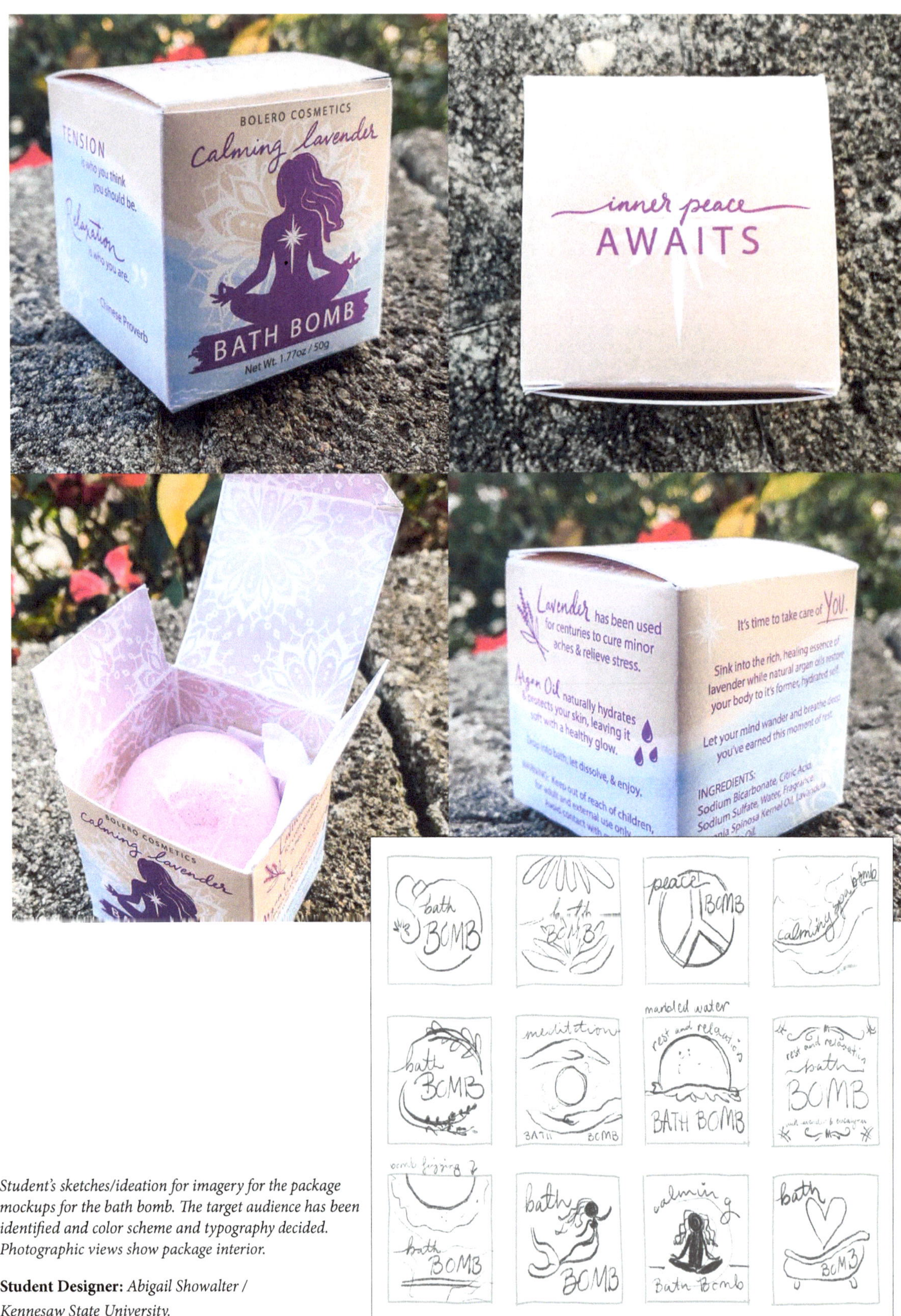

Student's sketches/ideation for imagery for the package mockups for the bath bomb. The target audience has been identified and color scheme and typography decided. Photographic views show package interior.

Student Designer: *Abigail Showalter / Kennesaw State University.*

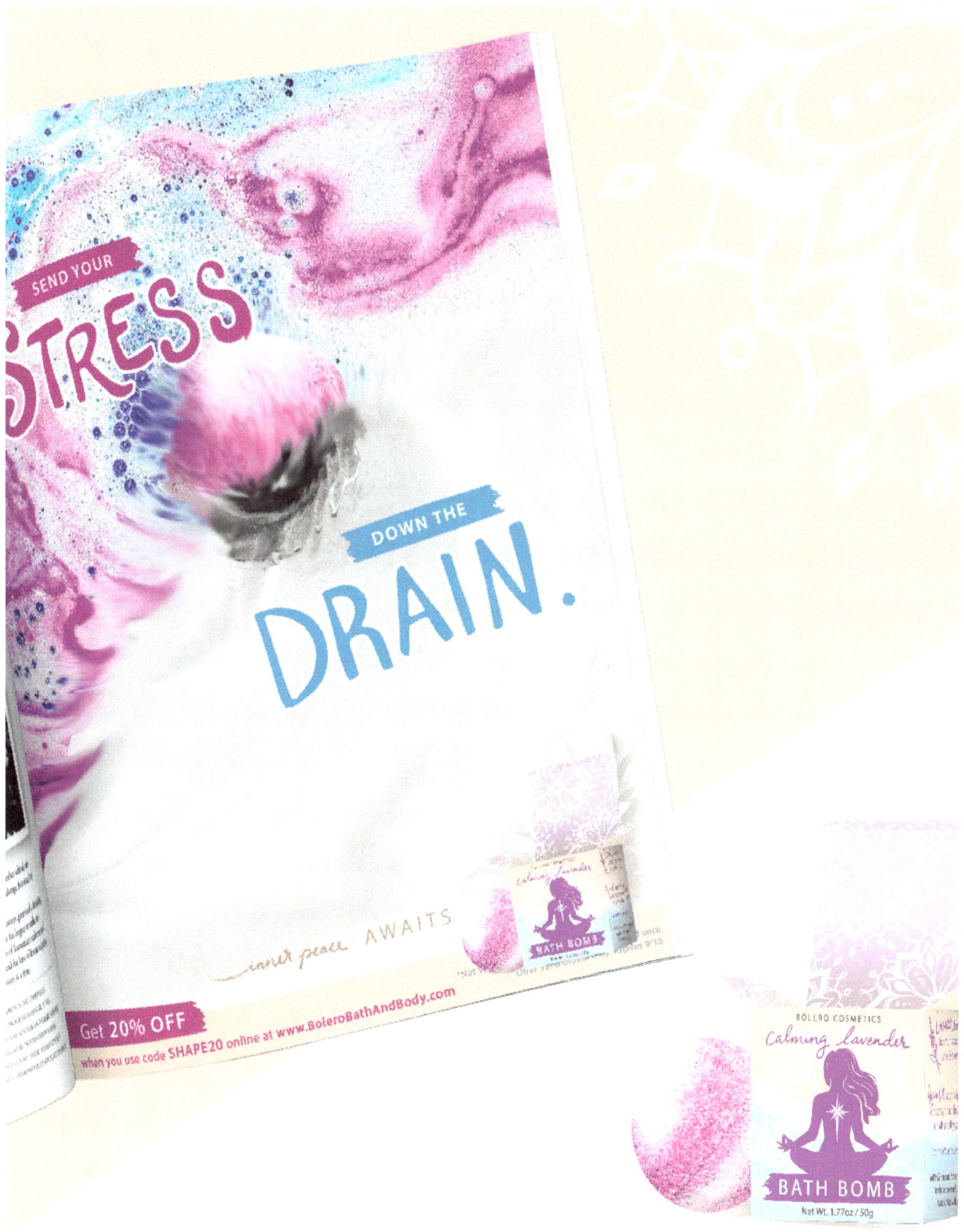

Student presentation of the creative ad for the bath bomb placed in a magazine geared towards the specific target audience.
Student has used the product as the sign-off in the ad. Notice how the design element on the inner packaging is also used in the ad.

Student Designer: *Abigail Showalter / Kennesaw State University.*

The Design Brief: Create a 12-page magazine for a spa that reflects the spa's brand and appeals to the target audience by promoting relaxation, wellness, and beauty. This magazine should showcase various spa treatments, services, and packages with visually appealing images and clear descriptions. Examples of these offerings could include massages, facials, body treatments, and special promotions. The magazine should be designed to be a takeaway gift.

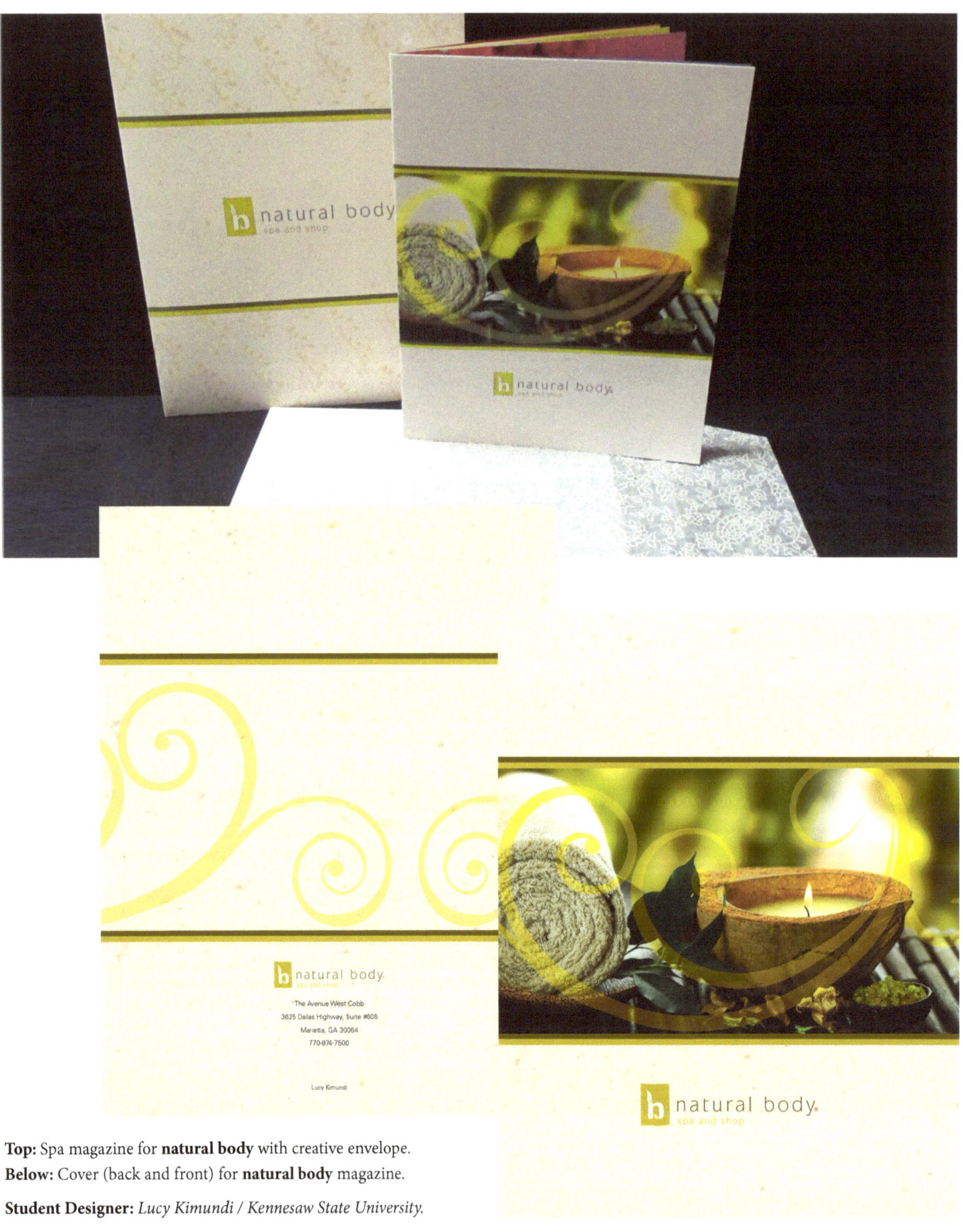

Top: Spa magazine for **natural body** with creative envelope.
Below: Cover (back and front) for **natural body** magazine.

Student Designer: *Lucy Kimundi / Kennesaw State University.*

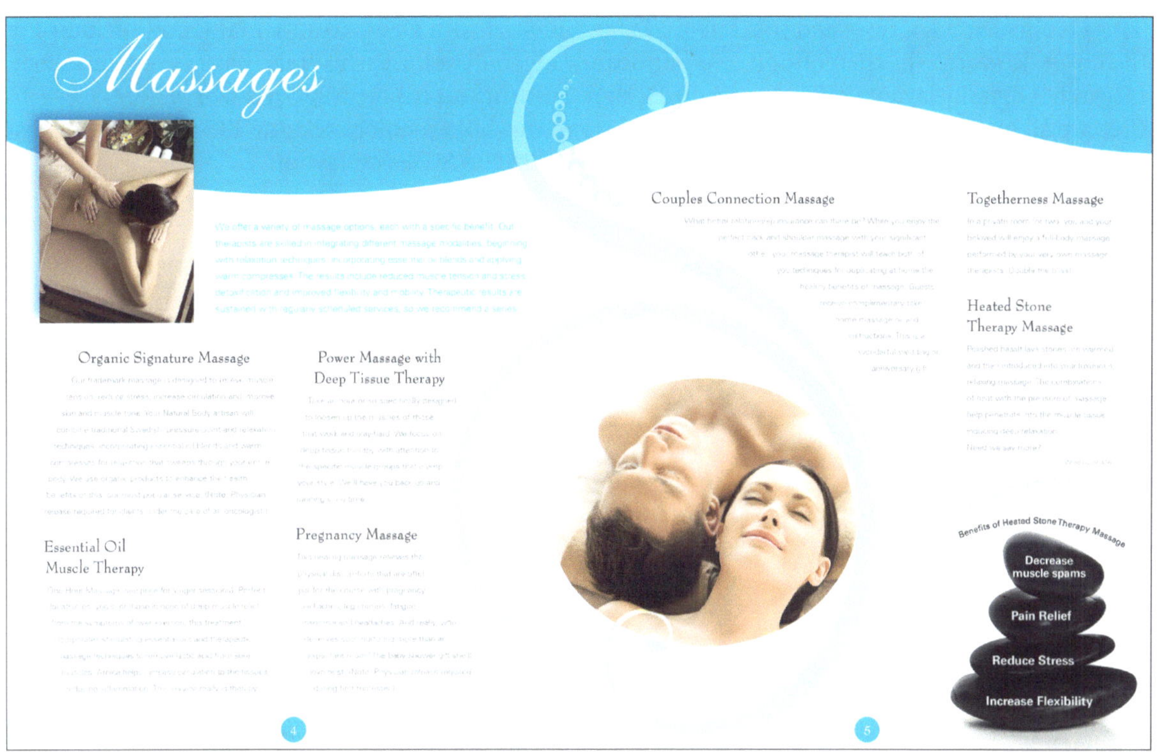

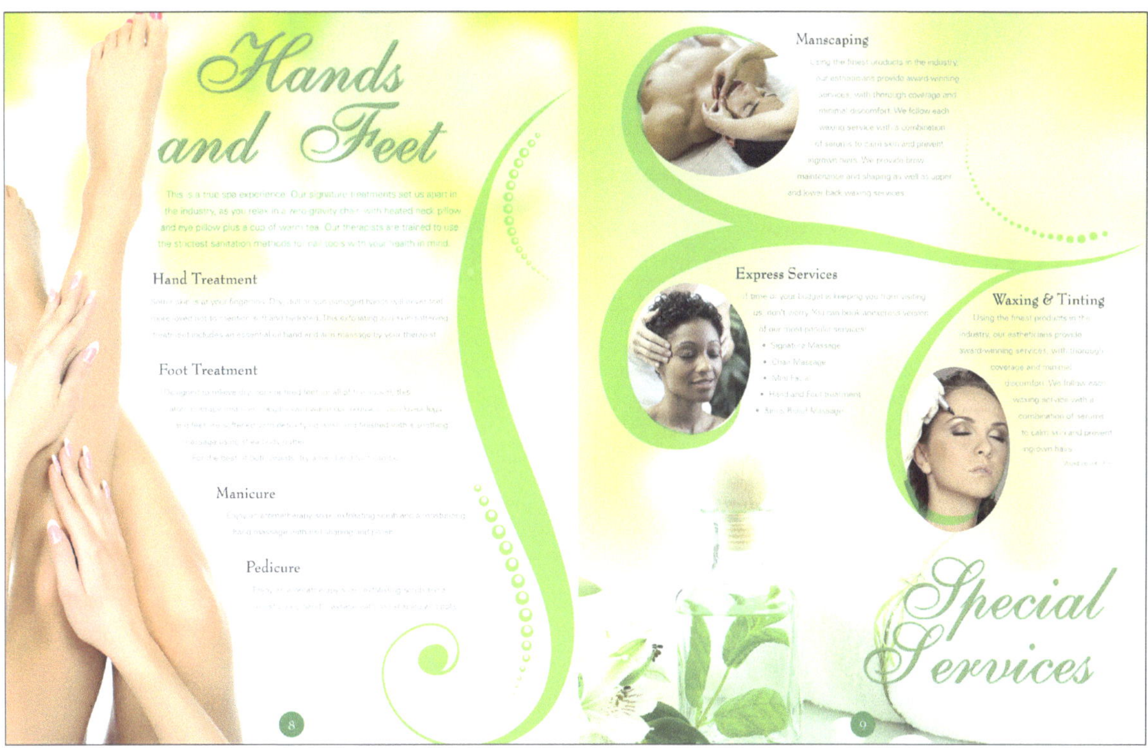

Two page-spreads from the **natural body** spa magazine.
Stock images were purchased and used for the magazine.

Student Designer: *Lucy Kimundi / Kennesaw State University.*

The Design Brief: Create and mockup a 12-page booklet with an environmental focus, including the cover. Research the theme/topic and hand-draw all content for each spread based on your image research. Digitally layout each spread in InDesign, ensuring bleeds are included where necessary. Prepare all images in Photoshop and/or Illustrator in the CMYK color mode at 300 ppi. Images must be sized correctly in Photoshop to fit the desired areas in the InDesign layout.

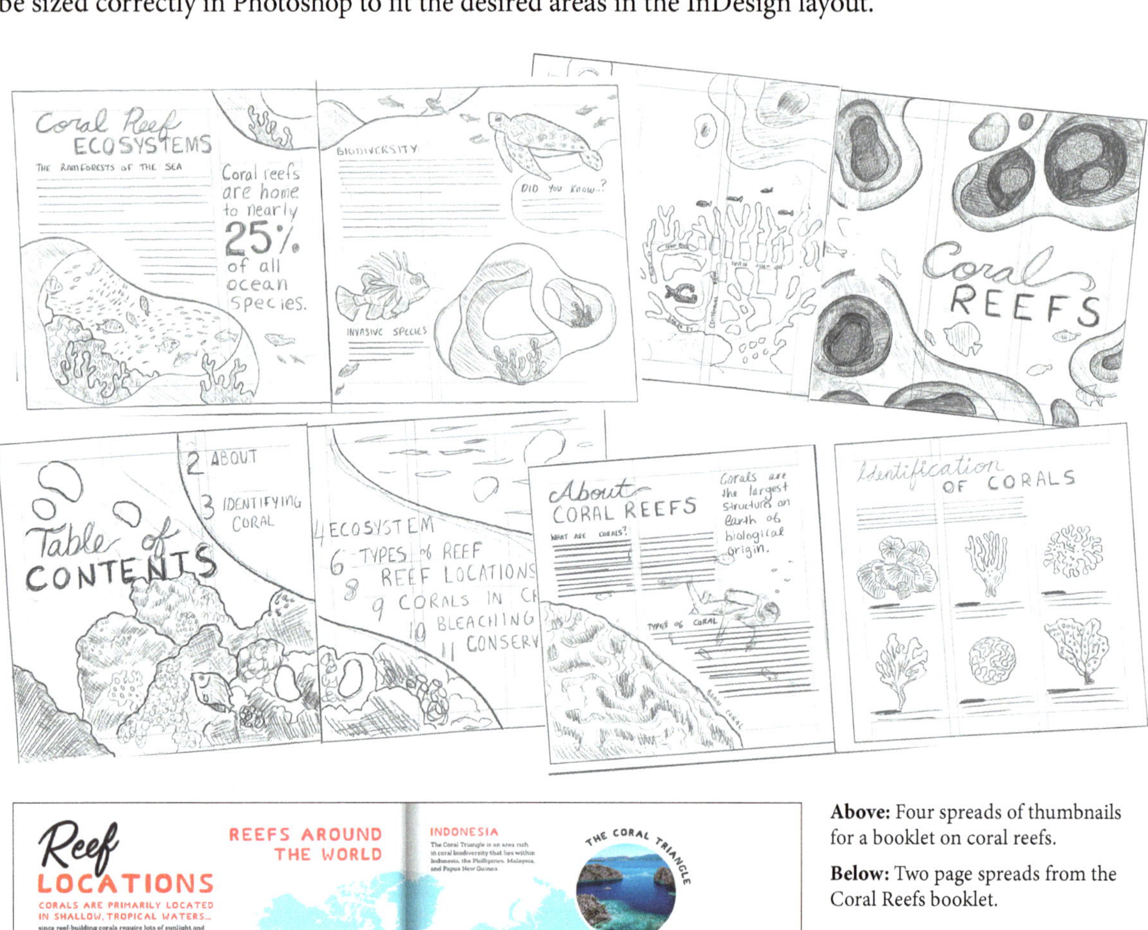

Above: Four spreads of thumbnails for a booklet on coral reefs.

Below: Two page spreads from the Coral Reefs booklet.

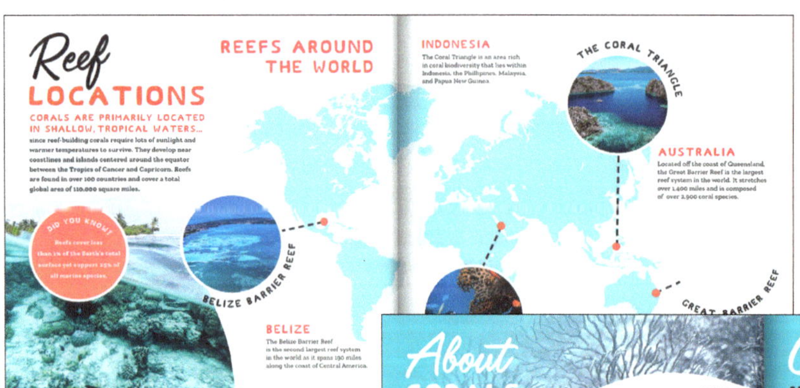

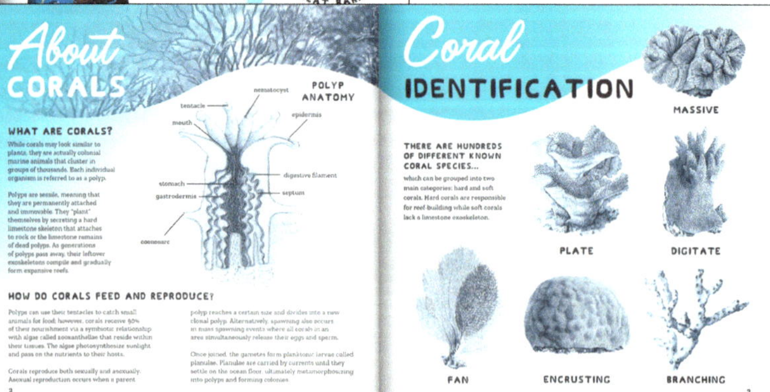

Note that during the digital development stage, design revisions to the layout are common for achieving visual cohesiveness.

Student Designer: *Savannah Winn / Kennesaw State University.*

The Design Brief: Create and mock up your restaurant's annual report. Develop working thumbnails for all content for each spread, based on design content. Digitally layout all content in InDesign, including bleeds where necessary. Minor deviations from the thumbnails are permitted.

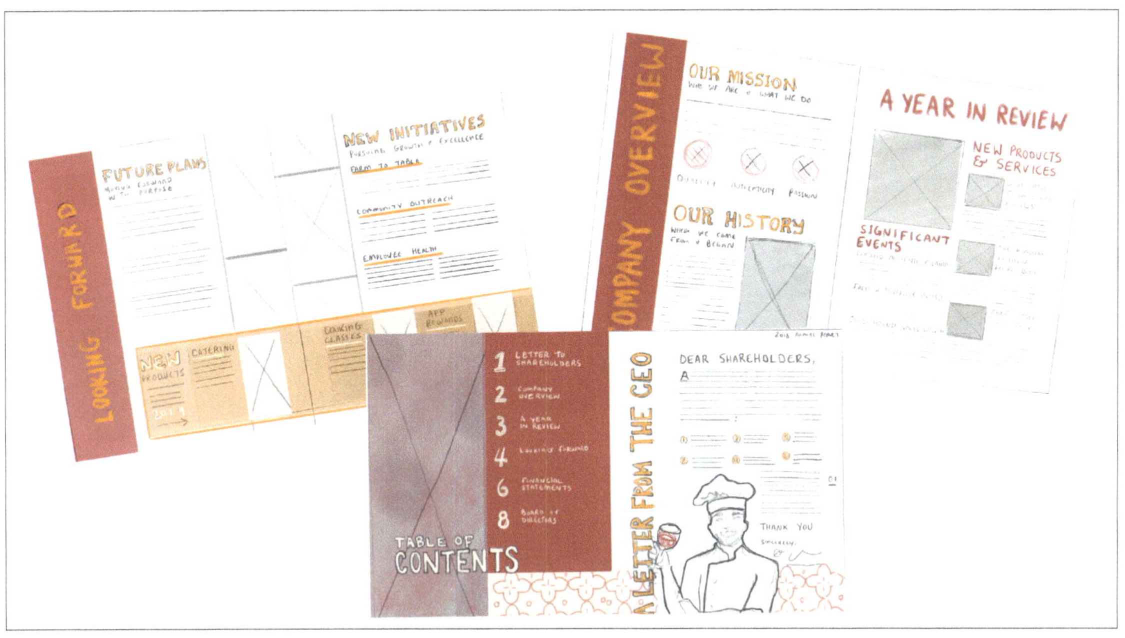

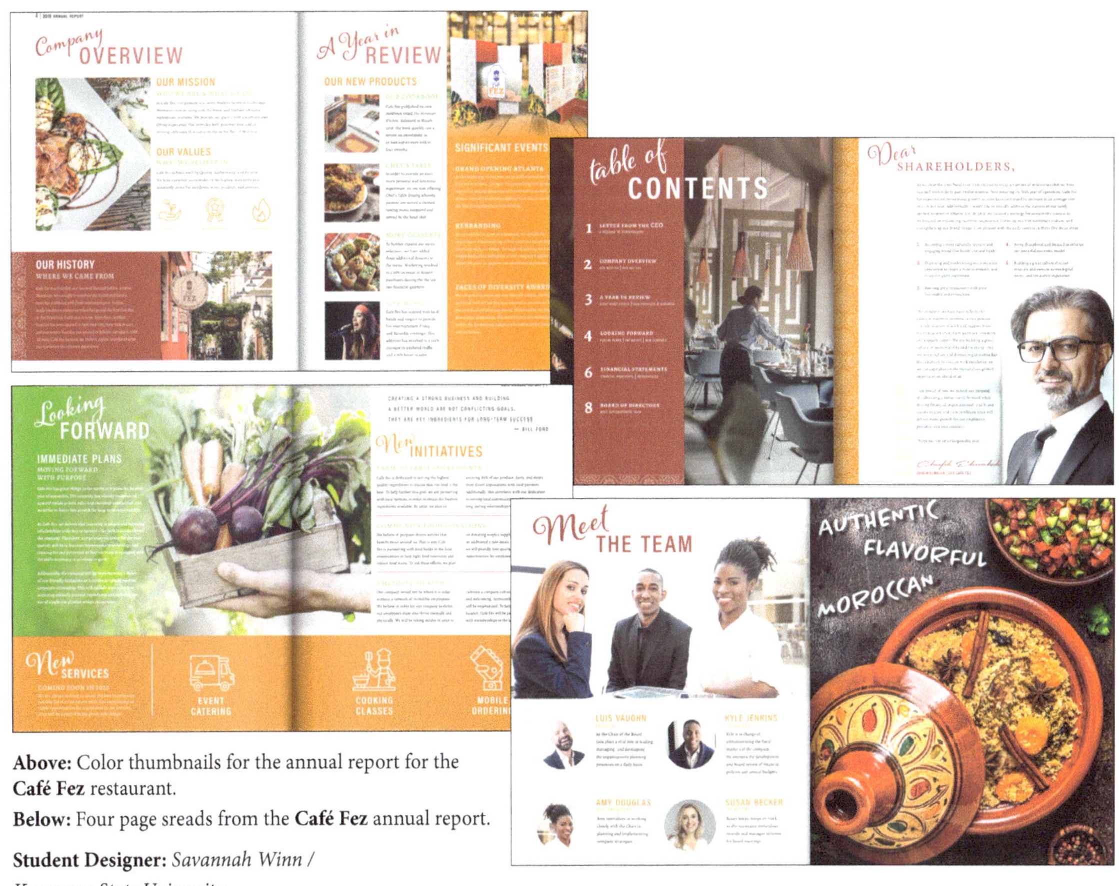

Above: Color thumbnails for the annual report for the **Café Fez** restaurant.

Below: Four page sreads from the **Café Fez** annual report.

Student Designer: *Savannah Winn /*
Kennesaw State University.

A STUDENT'S DESIGN SOLUTIONS FOR A RESTAURANT BRAND

This design problem involved creating a strong and effective well-defined restaurant brand to help establish a unique identity, attract customers, and build loyalty. Though not in Rome, the branding and cuisine are Roman-inspired, intended for an audience interested in history and who want their restaurant dining to be an experience, not just another meal.

Here's how one student created a memorable logo with a distinct and recognizable visual, a color scheme, and chose typography that complemented the brand's image and voice across all touchpoints of the branding and marketing.

Student Designer: Kyla Resnick - *Graduate of Kennesaw State University.*
Follow Kyla's design journey to the presentation of the final brand items for the Olympus restaurant branding from the logo and its application to stationery, the restaurant menu, recipe book, and annual report. *(A GDUSA Award winner).*

The Design Brief
Develop creative branding for a new Italian restaurant *Olympus*. This new, upscale Italian restaurant is inspired by the temples of the gods and goddesses of Ancient Rome. The name comes from Mount Olympus, believed to be the home of the gods and goddesses.

Process
The process began with thorough brainstorming and research for inspiration followed by numerous thumbnail sketches and design ideation for the design of the restaurant's branding beginning with the logo which explored ancient Roman architectural columns, statues and buildings. (The actual process is not shown here).

1. the logo
2. corporate business cards
3. corporate letterhead and envelope for printed correspondence
4. restaurant menu
5. annual report

The logo design:

The main idea in creating this logo is that it was to become the key brand mark to use on all the marketing materials for the restaurant. Concepts were explored around the Greek columns in ancient Greek architecture as a part of the brand image and marketing strategy. The image of the Ionic Greek column emerged as the main visual and its implementation became the image and voice for the brand.

The logo is a blend of a fork and a column, taken from the columns in front of the gods' temples. The dots between the letters in the word "Olympus" are inspired by interpuncts, which were used as word seperators in big lettering on temples. The typeface is reminiscent of Ancient Roman lettering. The grayish blue color is taken from the marble and stone from which the temples and statues are made.

Follow Kyla's design journey to the final presentation of the brand items for the Olympus restaurant branding.

Note that the main brand mark, a vector image, was purchased from an image bank which allowed for the editing of purchased images without attribution. In some instances, the ideal image can be acquired from an image bank during research, as was the case in this instance. The vector image was then converted to outlines in Adobe Illustrator. The designer then edited the outer vertical strokes of the fork shape at an inward angle. The word "MAGNA" was replaced with the restaurant's name, "OLYMPUS" and the designer explored several options for the background from flat color to imagery. Other elements in the logo could suggest table items.

Three finished ideas were presented for communication with the client to discuss the general directions and approval for meeting the client's expectations. Once the logo and color scheme were approved by the client, the designer finalized the logo, and its application to other touchpoints of the brand was explored.

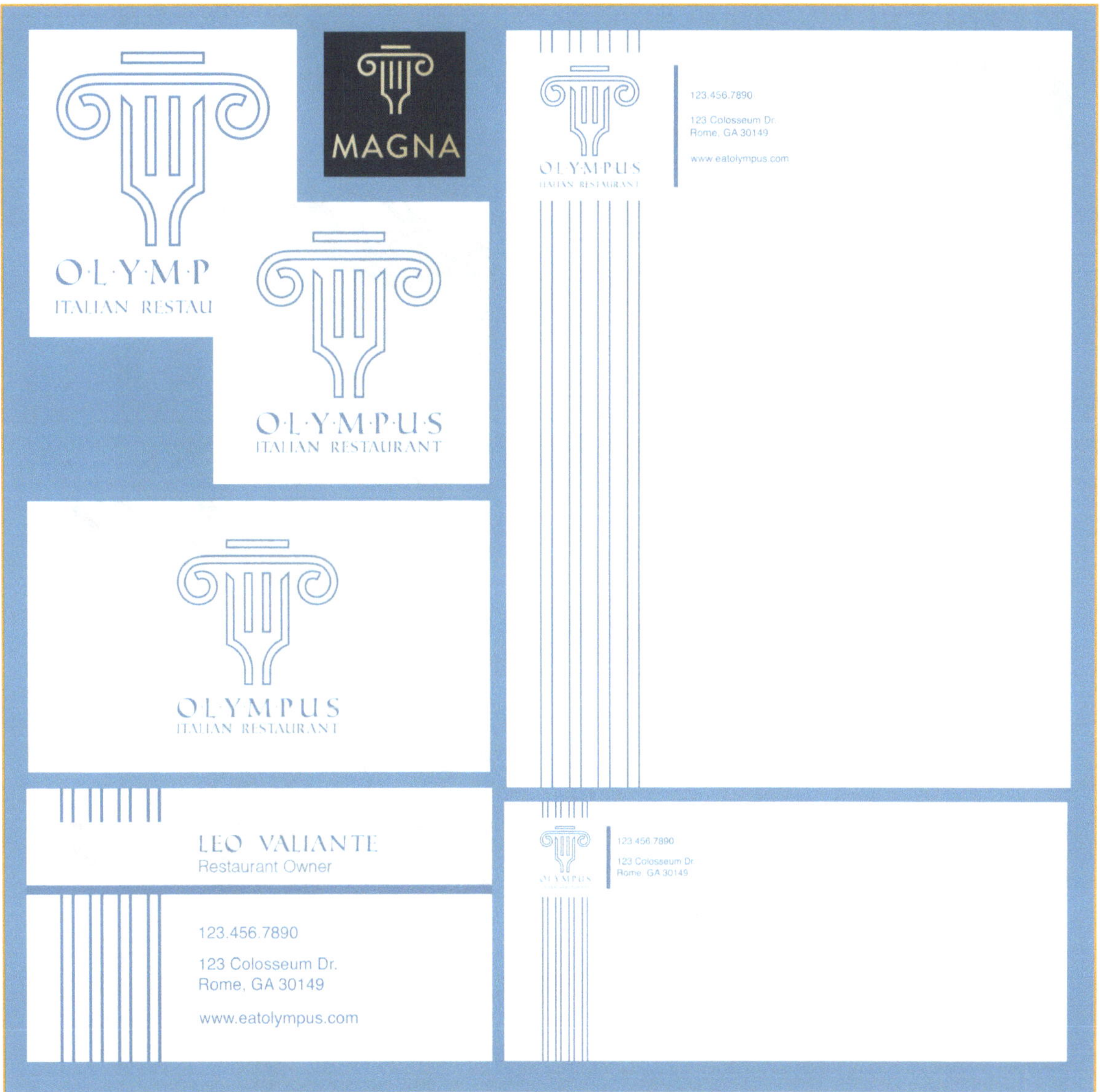

Presentation of the logo, business card, letterhead and envelope for Olympus restaurant brand.
The concept of the image as a fork is clever.
Student Designer: *Kyla Resnick / Kennesaw State University.*

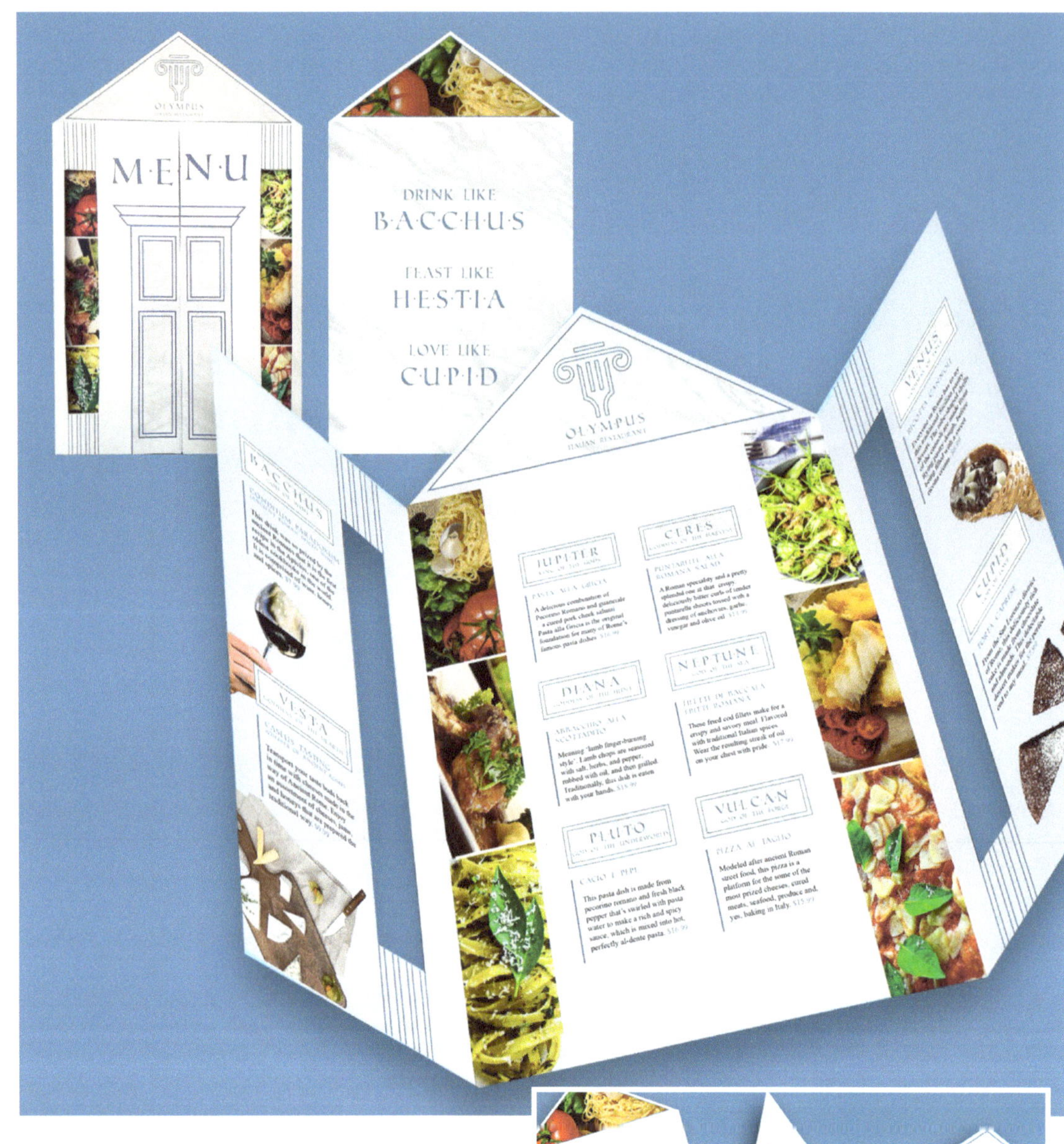

Olympus Restaurant Menu design.

The concept of the open door serves as a welcoming invitation to enter to partake of the sumptuous cuisine seen through the cut-outs that suggests the Greek architectural columns at the sides of the door.

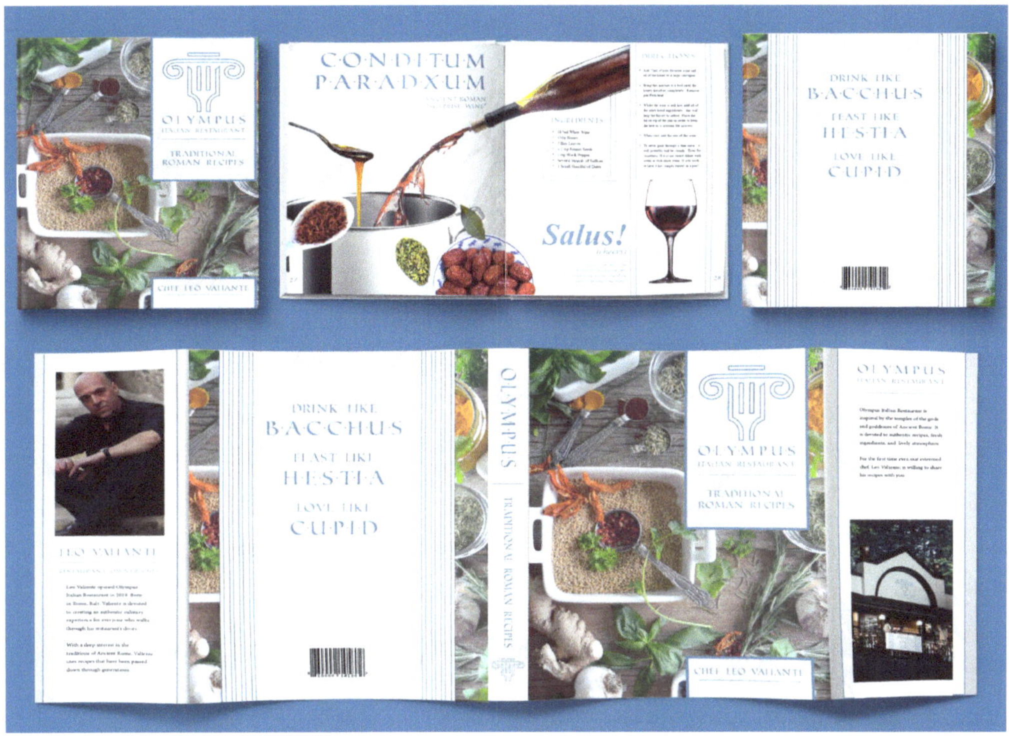

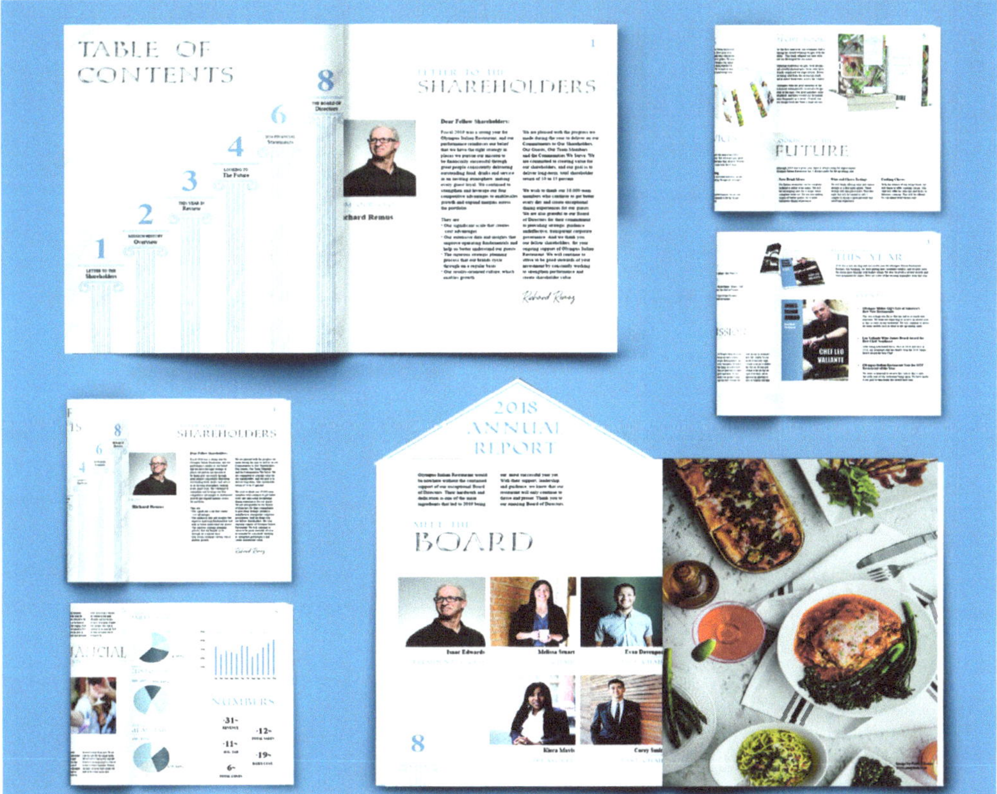

Above: *Olympus* restaurant recipe book open to show recipes named after the gods/godesses: Baccus, Hestia, Cupid.
Below: *Olympus* restaurant annual report showing several spreads. Note the Table of Contents use of the columns with snippets of the marble element to reinforce the branding.

STUDENT DESIGN SOLUTIONS FOR A NEW PERFUME BRAND

The Design Brief:

Develop creative branding for a new scent of perfume, along with a shopping bag specific to the brand. Begin by identifying your target market before research begins. Students brainstormed in teams to help each other identify target markets before selecting one for their perfume product. Create visually cohesive mockups for both the perfume package and shopping bag. These were the steps to help guide the students through the process:

Understand the Brand and Target Audience: Start by getting a clear understanding of the brand identity, values, and target audience for the perfume. Consider the brand's position in the market, its personality, and the preferences of its target consumers.

Conduct Market Research: Research current trends and competitors in the perfume industry. Analyze popular bottle designs, packaging styles, and branding strategies to identify opportunities for differentiation and innovation.

Sketch and Brainstorm Ideas: Consider how the bottle design can reflect the brand's identity, evoke emotions, and stand out on the shelf.

Consider Ergonomics and Functionality: Pay attention to the ergonomics and functionality of the bottle design. Ensure that the bottle is comfortable to hold, easy to use, and suitable for the chosen application method (spray, roll-on, etc.).

Select Materials and Finishes: Choose materials and finishes that align with the brand image and product positioning. Consider factors like transparency, opacity, texture, weight, and durability when making your selections.

Integrate Branding Elements: Incorporate branding elements such as logos, typography, colors, and graphics into the overall design. Make sure that the branding is cohesive with the overall brand identity and reinforces brand recognition.

Prototype and Test Designs: Create prototypes for the bottle's package and the shopping bag. Test the prototypes for functionality, aesthetics, and consumer appeal.

Refine the product: Based on feedback and testing results, refine the package and bag designs to address any issues or concerns and improve the overall design. Make adjustments to the shape, proportions, details, and branding elements as needed.

Prepare for Presentation: Remember to consider the packaging and presentation of the perfume bottle, including outer packaging, labels, inserts, and display materials. Ensure that the packaging complements the bottle design and enhances the overall product experience.

Remember to be mindful of regulatory requirements and industry standards for perfume packaging, including safety, labeling, and environmental considerations.

By following these steps and combining creativity, market research, and technical expertise, you can embark on the design process for a perfume bottle and create a visually stunning and commercially successful product that resonates with consumers.

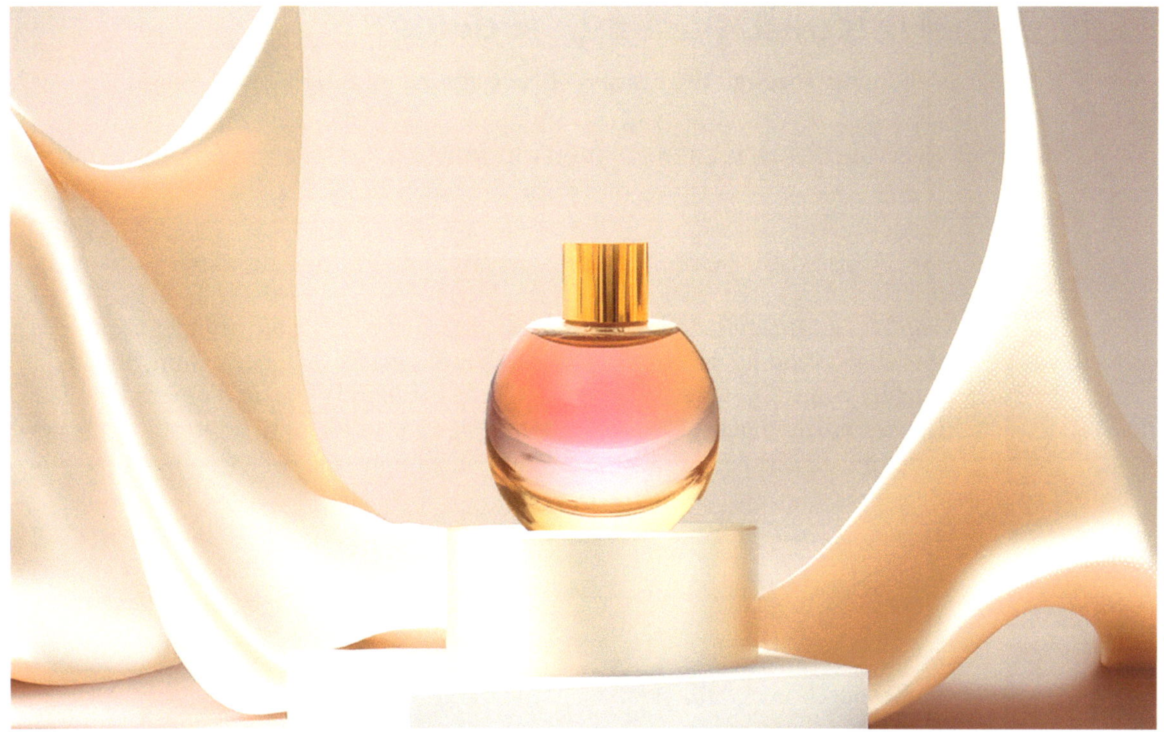

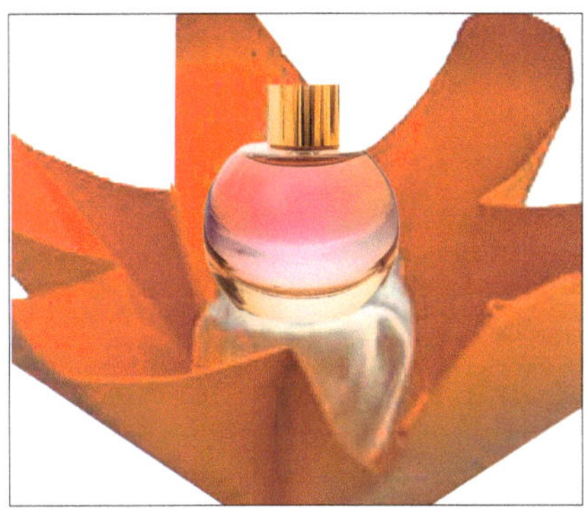

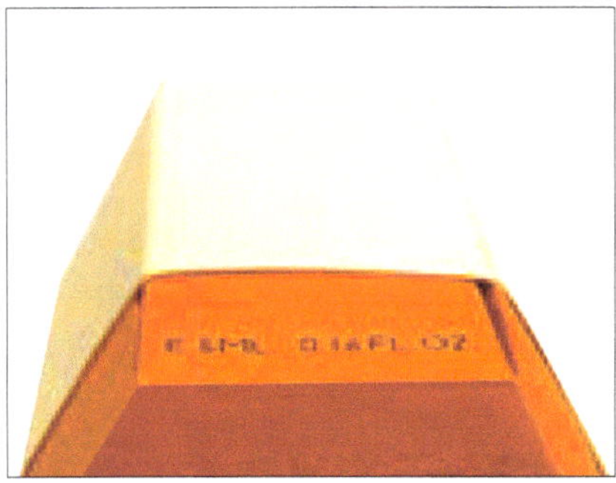

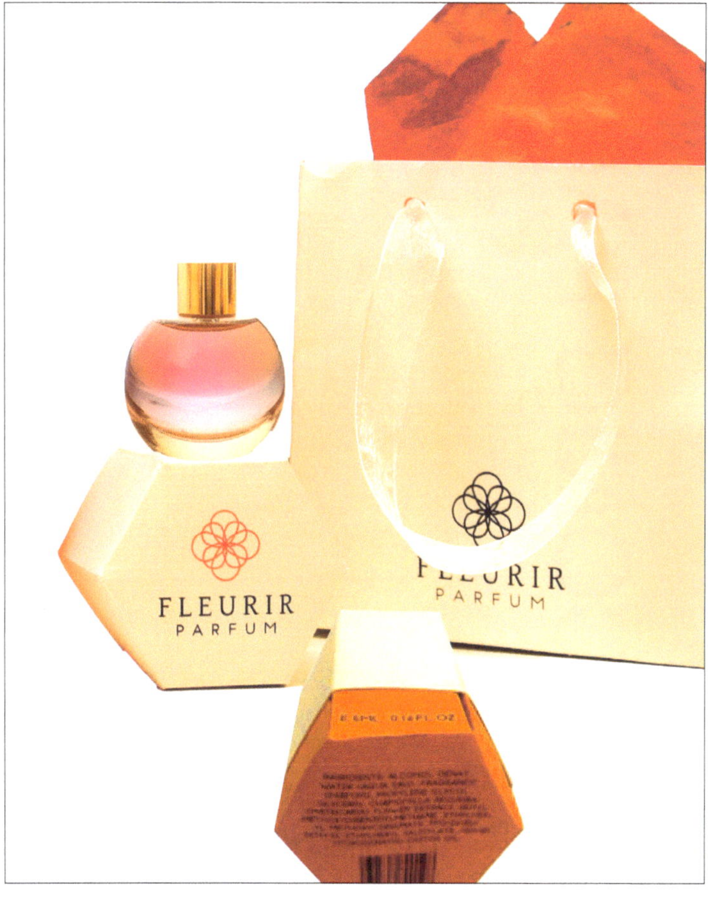

Perfume brand design for FLEURIR Parfum. Student created and presented a visually stunning and commercially successful product showing excellent craftsmanship.

Student Designer: *Celianne Pianeta / Kennesaw State University.*

YOUR FIRST CHALLENGE
AN ICONIC PACKAGE REDESIGN

An iconic package redesign

(A journey through the process of redesigning an existing package).

Every challenge is an opportunity to learn and grow as a designer. Embrace the process, stay curious, and approach each design task with a positive and determined mindset. Read the brief, pay attention to the details, and manage your time. Don't be afraid to explore unconventional ideas.and solutions.

The Design Brief: Redesign an existing package for an iconic product usually found in a vending machine (e.g. Welch's Fruit Snacks, Wrigley's Gum, Snicker's, Keebler Animal Crackers Snack, etc.). Keep the brand's logo and other identifiers (for the mockup purposes only). Then design a creative ad to reintroduce the newly redesigned packaged product. Remember the importance of engaging in the process.

Here are the key steps the to take throughout your redesign journey:

PART A:

1. Research and Analysis:
Conduct a thorough analysis of the current package design, considering its strengths and perceived weaknesses. Identify areas for improvement. Research will entail purchasing and trying the product.

2. Define Objectives:
Clearly outline the goals of the redesign. You want to modernize the brand's image to improve visibility when placed into the vending machine.

3. Understand the Target Audience:
Identify and understand the target demographic for the product, considering preferences, lifestyles, and purchasing behaviors to tailor the redesign.

4. Competitive Analysis:
Competitors' packaging designs must be analysed to ensure the new design stands out and also identify opportunities for differentiation.

5. Concept Development:
Generate design concepts based on research findings and objectives. Explore the brand's visual elements, color schemes, typography, and imagery to convey the desired message.

6. Collaboration and Feedback:
Collaborate with group for feedback. Collect feedback on concepts to refine and align the design with intended goals.

7. Prototyping:
Create prototypes or mock-ups to visualize how the redesigned package will appear in a real-world context, and evaluate practicality and visual impact during this phase.

8. Testing:
Conduct testing to gather feedback on the redesigned package, and to assess how well it communicates the brand message, attracts attention, and meets the target audience preferences. At this point you can consider a survey with your social media groups or specific design community.

9. Refinement:
Based on feedback, refine the design, addressing concerns or suggestions to ensure the final package design meets brand and consumer expectations effectively.

10. Implementation:
Work to ensure successful implementation of the final design. Print on appropriate stock (paper). Photograph at least 3-5 different views for selection to place in your portfolio.

PART B:

Design the creative ad for the newly repackaged product. Begin by researching the elements of an ad.

1. Define the Ad's Objectives

2. Gather Visual Assets

3. Choose Design Software

4. Set Up Document

5. Highlight Key Features

6. Brainstorm and Develop a Compelling Headline

7. Incorporate Branding

8. Use Engaging Copy

9. Design Layout and Composition

10. Implement a Color Scheme

11. Consider the sign-off

12. Test and Refine

13. Finalize and Export

14. Launch and Monitor

By following these steps, you can design a compelling mock up and a creative advertisement that effectively showcases the newly designed packaged product and capture the attention of your target audience. Deciding how you're going to test is crucial. Maybe at a school with vending machines from which the students regularly purchase the products, or among your social media community.

A PORTFOLIO OF YOUR DESIGN MOCKUPS

You should now be ready to begin the creation of a portfolio of well-crafted mockups for effectively showcasing your skills. A well-designed portfolio acts as a visual resume, enabling potential clients or employers to evaluate your design style, creativity, and technical expertise.

Let's explore the key reasons why you should invest in building a portfolio of your mockups:

Showcase Your Skills: A portfolio is a platform to demonstrate your design abilities. By including mockup projects, you can highlight your proficiency in creating realistic and visually appealing presentations for various design concepts.

Demonstrate Diverse Capabilities: Including a range of mockup projects in your portfolio allows you to showcase your versatility. Whether it's product packaging, website interfaces, or branding materials, different mockups can demonstrate your ability to adapt to various design challenges.

Highlight Problem-Solving Abilities: Mockup projects often involve addressing specific design challenges, such as layout, color schemes, and user interactions. Your portfolio can illustrate how you approach and creatively solve these challenges. Include a brief story about the intent of the project and how your design(s) solved the problem.

Tell a Story: A portfolio tells a visual story of your design journey. It can convey your design evolution, the progression of skills, and the diversity of projects you've undertaken. This narrative can engage viewers and leave a lasting impression.

Attract Potential Clients or Employers: A portfolio is a powerful tool for attracting opportunities. A well-curated collection of mockup projects can make you stand out in a competitive field.

Build Credibility: A portfolio establishes your credibility as a designer. It provides evidence of your past work and serves as a testament to your abilities, helping to build trust with potential clients or employers.

Create an Online Presence: In today's digital age, having an online portfolio allows you to reach a global audience. Platforms like Behance, Dribbble, or your personal website provide spaces to showcase your mockups to a wide audience.

Receive Constructive Feedback: A portfolio is not just a presentation tool; it's also an opportunity to receive feedback from peers, mentors, or potential clients. Constructive feedback can help you refine your skills and improve your future projects.

Remember that the effectiveness of a mockup depends on the context and the intended audience. Experiment with different mockupss, seek feedback, and refine your designs based on the principles of visual hierarchy, balance, and consistency. As you gain experience, you'll develop an intuitive sense of what works best for different projects and design scenarios, and your mockups will begin to improve.

Tips to consider when creating your mockup portfolio

Curate Your Best Work: Select projects that showcase your strengths and best represent your design style.

Provide Context: Include brief descriptions for each project, explaining the concept, challenges faced, and solutions implemented.

Update Regularly: Keep your portfolio current by adding new mockup projects as you complete them. This reflects your ongoing commitment to growth and improvement.

Organize Effectively: Structure your portfolio in a way that is easy to navigate, allowing viewers to explore your work seamlessly.

Showcase Process: If possible, include insights into your design process. This can help potential clients or employers understand how you approach projects and solve design problems. In essence, how you engage in design thinking.

What type of portfolio should a graphic designer present?

Website portfolio: The most popular type of graphic design portfolio is the website portfolio. With a website portfolio, you can showcase a selection of your previous work online.

PDF portfolio: Another option for a graphic design portfolio is a portfolio in PDF format. This type of portfolio resembles a brochure in style.

Book portfolio: Graphic designers also have the option of creating a traditional book-style portfolio.

Here are a few links to graphic design portfolios online:

This is an Adobe portfolio (paste link into your browser).
https://portfolio.adobe.com/

FORMAT is a website portfolio builder for designers (paste link into your browser).
https://www.format.com/

Portfolio Box is an online portfolio website builder (paste link into your browser).
https://www.portfoliobox.net/

Remember that investing time and effort in developing a comprehensive mockup portfolio is a valuable investment in your graphic design career. Always include a brief story about the intent of the project and how your design solved the problem. Not only does it function as a showcase of your work, but it also positions you as a skilled and professional designer in the eyes of your audience and your competition. Remember to be consistent with typography throughout.

Inspiration for design mockups using online templates

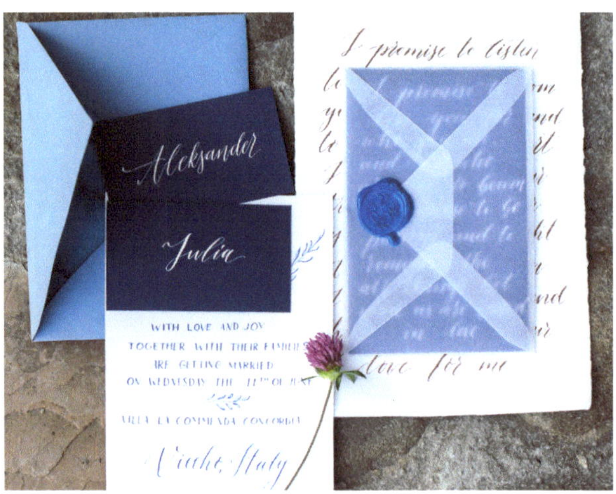

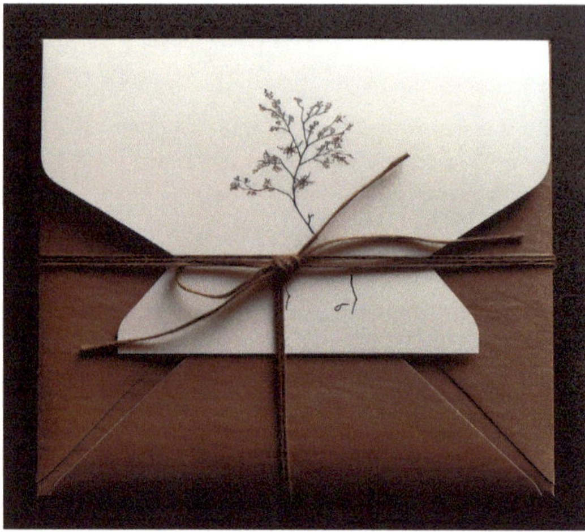

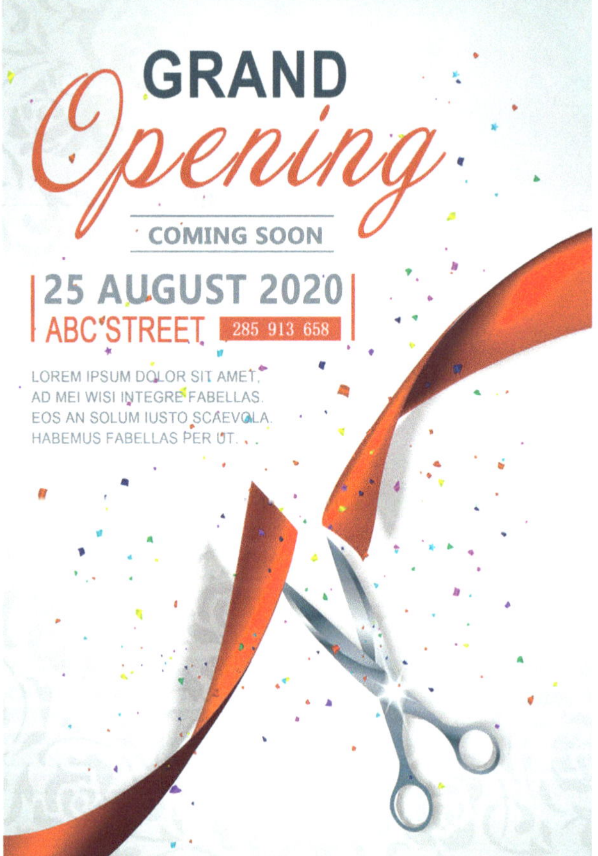

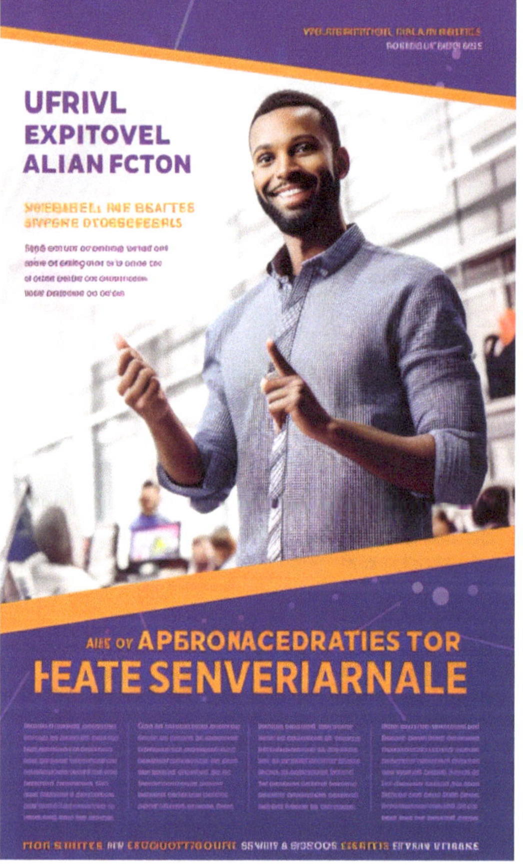

This page showcases various mockups that can serve as great inspiration for portfolio pieces in any language. You can easily find photos and vector graphics on popular image banks like Shutterstock, iStock, Vecteezy, and more. These platforms offer a wide range of templates for creating invitations, posters, announcements, newsletters, and one-of-a kind package designs among others. Additionally, you can conveniently purchase specialty paper, cardstock with different textures, and envelopes in various colors and sizes from online retailers such as The Paper Mill, Paper Source, LCI Paper, and others. Simply replace the existing images and text with your own to personalize your designs.

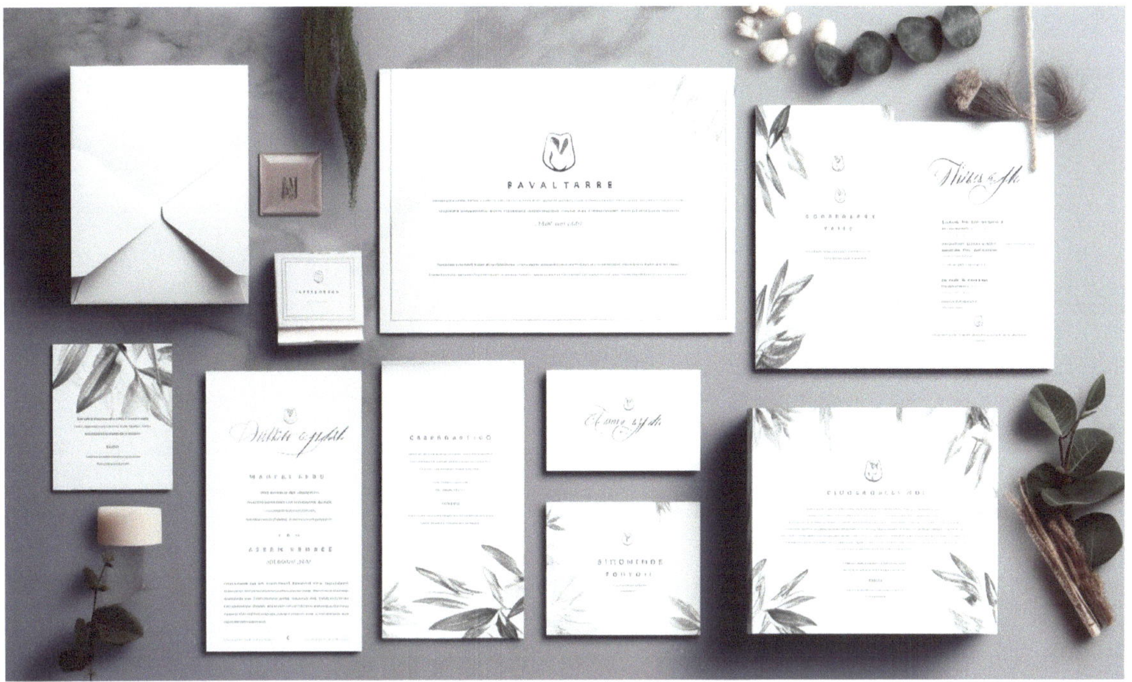

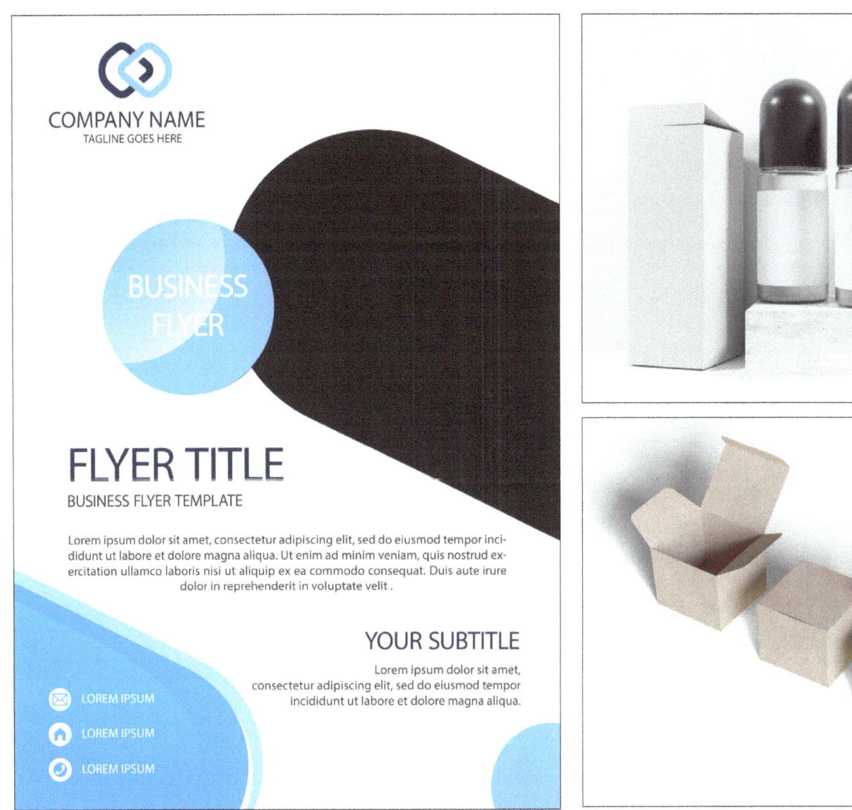

Explore online templates for wedding packages, flyers, bottle labels, and boxes to find inspiration for your mockups. These templates can serve as excellent portfolio pieces. Begin by identifying templates that can effectively communicate your message. Then, customize the text with your own content, in any language. Furthermore, try out different typefaces that align with your intended audience, message, and tone. Remember to replace or enhance any images as needed, and provide attribution when necessary. Lastly, carefully consider design principles such as balance, alignment, contrast, white space, and more.

Where can I find free design project briefs?

Finding free design project briefs can be challenging, but several online resources offer templates or examples.

Here are some places to search:

Online Design Communities:

Platforms like Behance, Dribbble, and DesignCrowd feature project case studies that may include project briefs or descriptions. Although they might not be labeled explicitly as briefs, you can still gain insights from the project details.

Open Source Platforms:

Explore open-source platforms like GitHub where designers sometimes share their projects, including accompanying documentation that may contain project briefs.

Educational Institutions:

University websites, design schools, and online learning platforms occasionally provide project briefs as part of design courses. Check for design course materials that include sample project briefs.

Freelance Platforms:

Websites like Upwork or Fiverr display project descriptions from clients seeking design services. While not comprehensive, these descriptions offer insights into client expectations.

Design Blogs and Websites:

Visit design blogs, websites, and forums where professionals share their experiences, including project briefs or descriptions. Look for platforms that offer real-world project insights.

Creative Agencies:

Some creative agencies or design studios share case studies on their websites, providing information on design processes and client collaborations.

Design Templates Websites:

Platforms like Canva or Adobe Stock offer design templates, including sample project brief templates that can be customized to suit your needs.

Remember while searching for project briefs, you must be aware that not all projects are publicly shared due to confidentiality agreements. If you cannot find specific briefs, consider resources that can guide you in creating effective design project briefs. Developing your template based on project requirements can be a valuable practice for your design workflow.

Do I need a website to market my design mockups?

Having a website can greatly improve your ability to market your mockups and establish a professional online presence as a graphic designer.

There are several reasons why having a website can be beneficial:

Centralized Portfolio: A website serves as a centralized platform where you can showcase your mockup projects. It provides a curated space for potential clients and employers to view your work, learn about your skills, and understand your design style.

Professional Image: A well-designed website conveys professionalism and helps you make a positive first impression. It reflects your commitment to your craft and attention to detail, which can instill confidence in potential clients.

Customization and Branding: With your own website, you have complete control over the design, layout, and branding. This allows you to create a personalized and cohesive online presence that aligns with your unique style and message.

Contact Information and Inquiries: A website provides a convenient way for people to get in touch with you. Include a contact page with your email, social media links, or a contact form, making it easy for potential clients to reach out and inquire about your services.

SEO and Visibility: Having a website allows you to optimize for search engines (SEO), making it easier for people to find you online. This can increase your visibility and attract a wider audience interested in graphic design services.

Blog or Insights Section: A blog or insights section on your website gives you the opportunity to share your thoughts, design process, and industry insights. Regularly publishing content can help establish you as an authority in your niche and improve your website's SEO.

Client Testimonials: Showcase client testimonials on your website to build credibility and trust. Positive feedback from satisfied clients can influence potential clients' decisions to work with you.

Personal Domain: Having your own domain name (e.g., www.yourname.com) adds a level of professionalism and makes it easier for people to remember and find you online.

Adaptability: Your website can evolve with your career. As you gain more experience and diversify your services, you can update your website to reflect these changes.

Online Porfolio Link: If you're just starting, you can use website builders or platforms like WordPress, Wix, or Squarespace to create a professional website without extensive coding knowledge. Include a dedicated section for your mockup projects, along with information about your skills, services, and contact details. And, create a direct link to your online portfolio.

Remember that while a website is a valuable tool, it's not the only way to market your mockups. Utilize social media platforms, design communities, and other online channels to share your work and connect with potential clients. Remember, the key is to have a cohesive online presence that effectively communicates your skills and showcases your best work.

Finding a niche in graphic design can be a strategic move that sets you apart from the competition and positions you as an expert in a specific area. Specializing in a niche allows you to tailor your skills and services to a particular audience, making your offerings more attractive to clients within that niche.

Some considerations to help you decide how to go about finding a niche:

Advantages of Finding a Niche:

Expertise and Authority: Specializing in a niche allows you to become an expert in a specific industry or type of design. This can build trust with clients who are looking for specialized knowledge.

Targeted Marketing: When you have a niche, your marketing efforts can be more focused. You can tailor your messaging and outreach to address the specific needs and pain points of your target audience.

Reduced Competition: In a niche, you may face less competition than in broader markets. This can make it easier to establish yourself and gain visibility.

Higher Rates: Clients often value specialists more and may be willing to pay higher rates for someone who understands their industry or specific design requirements.

How to Find Your Niche:

Evaluate Your Interests and Passions: Consider the types of projects or industries that genuinely excite and interest you. Your passion for a niche can drive your motivation and creativity.

Assess Your Skills: Identify your strengths and areas where you excel. Your unique skill set can be a valuable asset in a specific niche.

Research Market Demand: Investigate the demand for graphic design services within potential niches. Look for areas where there is a need for specialized design expertise.

Explore Industry Trends: Stay updated on trends within the design industry and potential niches. Emerging trends can present opportunities for specialization.

Identify Your Ideal Clients: Define the characteristics of your ideal clients. Understanding their needs, challenges, and preferences can help you choose a niche that aligns with your target audience.

Test and Refine: Experiment with different niches and projects. Pay attention to what resonates most with you and where you receive positive feedback. Iterate based on your experiences.

FIND A NICHE TO MARKET YOURSELF

Examples of Graphic Design Niches:

1. Branding and Logo Design: Specializing in creating memorable brand identities and logos for businesses.

2. Packaging Design: Focusing on designing product packaging for various industries.

3. Web and App Design: Becoming an expert in designing user interfaces and experiences for websites and applications.

4. Print and Editorial Design: Specializing in designing magazines, books, and other print materials.

5. Illustration: Concentrating on creating custom illustrations for a specific market, such as children's books or editorial illustrations.

6. Social Media Graphics: Providing design services specifically tailored for social media platforms.

Remember that finding a niche doesn't mean limiting yourself forever; it's about strategically positioning yourself in the market. As your career progresses, you may choose to expand or refine your niche based on changing interests, industry trends, or emerging opportunities.

Do I offer services for free when starting out?

Though not mandatory, offering services for free when starting out as a graphic designer can be a strategic decision, but it's essential to approach it thoughtfully and set boundaries. Professionally, it is advised that you not work for free for any one client or too many clients for too long. Many designers start by charging reasonable rates from the beginning. If you choose this route, ensure that your pricing reflects the value of your skills and the effort you put into each project.

Here are some reasons why offering free services might be considered, along with important considerations:

Reasons to Offer Free Services:

Build Your Portfolio: If you're just starting, having a portfolio with real-world examples of your work is crucial. Offering free services allows you to build a portfolio that showcases your skills and capabilities.

Gain Experience: Working on real projects, even if unpaid initially, provides valuable experience. It allows you to practice your skills, understand client expectations, and improve your workflow.

Establish a Reputation: Offering free services can help you establish a positive reputation in your network or community. Satisfied clients may provide testimonials, referrals, or can lead to paid opportunities in the future.

Networking Opportunities: Working for free can open doors to valuable networking opportunities. Building relationships with clients, even on unpaid projects, can lead to future collaborations or referrals.

Learn About Client Communication: Interacting with clients, understanding their needs, and effectively communicating throughout a project are skills that take time to develop. Free projects can serve as a low-pressure environment to hone these skills.

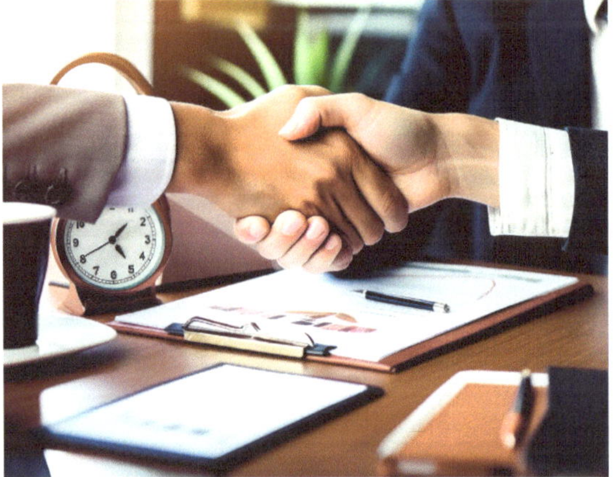
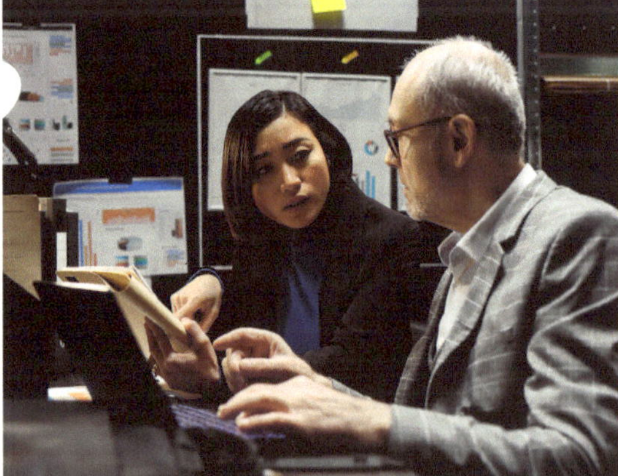

Effective client communication is crucial for the success of a service-based business.

Important considerations when starting out

Define Boundaries:
Clearly communicate the scope of the free services you are offering. Define the project's limitations, such as the number of revisions, deliverables, and the timeframe. Setting boundaries ensures that both you and the client have realistic expectations.

Choose Strategic Projects:
Select projects that align with your interests, goals, and the type of work you want to pursue in the future. Focus on projects that contribute to your portfolio and help you grow in your desired direction.

Time Management:
Be mindful of your time investment. While working for free can be beneficial, it's essential not to compromise your ability to earn a living. Balance free projects with paid work or other income streams.

Transition to Paid Work:
As you gain experience and build your portfolio, gradually transition to seeking paid opportunities. Value your skills and time, and recognize when it's appropriate to start charging for your services.

Evaluate the Opportunity:
Assess the potential benefits of each free project. Consider the client's reputation, the visibility the project might bring, and whether it aligns with your long-term goals. Not all free opportunities are equal, and it's crucial to choose wisely.

Remember that offering free services is just one approach, and it's not mandatory. Many designers start by charging reasonable rates from the beginning. If you choose this route, ensure that your pricing reflects the value of your skills and the effort you put into each project. Ultimately, the decision to offer free services should align with your individual goals, circumstances, and the specific opportunities that arise.

THE IMPORTANCE OF STUDYING GRAPHIC DESIGN HISTORY

Studying the history of graphic design is essential for designers as it offers valuable insights into past innovations, styles, and cultural contexts. By understanding the evolution of design, designers gain inspiration, develop critical thinking skills, and feel connected to a larger design community. Ultimately, this knowledge enhances their ability to create meaningful and timeless designs, fostering creativity and expanding their design vocabulary. Moreover, studying historical design practices helps designers develop a discerning eye and critical judgment. It equips designers with the knowledge, inspiration, and perspective needed to create meaningful, impactful, and timeless designs that resonate with audiences and stand the test of time.

In essence, studying the history of graphic design is not just an academic pursuit, but a vital aspect of professional growth and development. It is also crucial for designers to research, read, and study the work of renowned logo designers, typographers, and illustrators from around the world. If possible, taking a course in the history of graphic design or purchasing books on the topic from the recommended lists that follow, will further foster a mindset of continuous learning for the contributions of those who came before them and the collective legacy of design innovation. This sense of continuity and belonging enriches the designer's own practice and strengthens the bonds that unite designers across generations and cultures.

Various types of reading materials that graphic design students should consider:

Design History and Theory:

Study the history and theory of graphic design to understand its evolution and the principles that underpin it. Books such as *Designing with Type* by James Craig. *Graphic Design: A New History* by Stephen Eskilson and *Meggs' History of Graphic Design* by Philip B. Meggs are valuable resources.

Design Books and Publications:

Explore books written by renowned graphic designers and design theorists. Topics can include design principles, typography, layout, color theory, and the creative process. Notable titles include *The Elements of Typographic Style* by Robert Bringhurst and *Thinking with Type* by Ellen Lupton.

Design Magazines and Journals:

Subscribe to design magazines and journals to stay updated on industry trends, emerging designers, and critical discussions in the design community. Magazines like *Communication Arts, Print,* and *Eye Magazine* offer insightful articles and showcases of contemporary design work.

A list of books that cover various aspects of the history of graphic design:

"A History of Graphic Design" by Philip B. Meggs: Widely regarded as one of the definitive books on the subject, this comprehensive text provides an overview of the evolution of graphic design from its origins to the present day.

"Graphic Design: A New History" by Stephen J. Eskilson: This book offers a fresh perspective on the history of graphic design, exploring key movements, styles, and practitioners from the late 19th century to the digital age.

"Graphic Design: A Concise History" by Richard Hollis: In this concise yet insightful book, Hollis traces the development of graphic design through key movements, innovations, and practitioners, offering a succinct overview of the field's evolution.

"The History of Graphic Design" by Jens Müller and Julius Wiedemann: This visually stunning book presents a chronological survey of graphic design history, featuring hundreds of examples of iconic works and influential designers from around the world.

"A History of Graphic Design for Rainy Days" by Studio Dunbar: Written by renowned Dutch designer Gert Dumbar, this unconventional book takes readers on a journey through graphic design history, offering anecdotes, insights, and personal reflections along the way.

"100 Ideas that Changed Graphic Design" by Steven Heller and Veronique Vienne: This book explores the evolution of graphic design through a series of key ideas and innovations that have shaped the field, from the invention of movable type to the rise of digital technology.

 "Graphic Design: A Visual History" by Dr. Guy Julier: With over 700 illustrations, this visual history of graphic design provides a comprehensive overview of the field, exploring its cultural, social, and technological contexts from the 15th century to the present.

"The Moderns: Midcentury American Graphic Design" by Steven Heller and Greg D'Onofrio: Focusing on the mid-20th century period, this book celebrates the achievements of American graphic designers who revolutionized the field with their innovative approaches to typography, advertising, and branding.

"Designing Modern Britain" by Cheryl Buckley and Fiona Fisher: This book examines the role of graphic design in shaping modern British culture and identity, tracing its evolution from the Arts and Crafts movement to the postwar era of consumerism and mass media.

"The Graphic Design Reader" edited by Teal Triggs and Leslie Atzmon: This anthology brings together key texts and essays by leading thinkers and practitioners in the field of graphic design, offering diverse perspectives on its history, theory, and practice.

These books offer valuable insights into the history, evolution, and cultural significance of graphic design, making them essential reading for students, educators, and practitioners in the field

Iconic logo designers who have left an indelible mark on the field of graphic design

Paul Rand: Widely regarded as one of the pioneers of modern graphic design. He created iconic logos for companies such as IBM, ABC, UPS, and NeXT. His work emphasized simplicity, wit, and timeless design principles.

Milton Glaser: Best known for his "I❤NY" logo, he was a prolific graphic designer who also co-founded New York Magazine. His diverse body of work includes logos for companies like DC Comics, Brooklyn Brewery, and the Brooklyn Academy of Music.

Saul Bass: Renowned for his groundbreaking work in film title sequences, he also designed memorable logos for companies such as AT&T, United Airlines, and Minolta. His logos often featured bold, minimalist designs with a focus on symbolism and storytelling.

Paula Scher: A partner at the design firm Pentagram, she has created iconic logos for clients like Citibank, Tiffany & Co., and Microsoft Windows. Her bold, graphic style and use of typography have had a significant influence on contemporary logo design.

Walter Landor: Founder of the branding agency Landor Associates, he pioneered the concept of branding and created logos for companies such as Coca-Cola, FedEx, and Levi's. His approach emphasized the emotional connection between brands and consumers.

Ivan Chermayeff and Tom Geismar: Co-founders of the design firm Chermayeff & Geismar & Haviv, Ivan Chermayeff and Tom Geismar have collaborated on iconic logos for clients like Chase Bank, NBC, and Mobil. Their designs are known for their simplicity, versatility, and enduring appeal.

Massimo Vignelli: An influential designer known for his modernist approach, Massimo Vignelli created logos for companies such as American Airlines, Bloomingdale's, and IBM. His work is characterized by geometric forms, grid-based layouts, and the use of Helvetica typography.

Lindon Leader: Lindon Leader, the designer of the FedEx logo, is celebrated for his clever use of negative space to create a hidden arrow within the logo. His work demonstrates the power of simplicity and symbolism in effective logo design.

Michael Bierut: A partner at Pentagram, Michael Bierut has designed logos for clients such as Verizon, MIT Media Lab, and Saks Fifth Avenue. His designs are known for their clarity, intelligence, and ability to distill complex ideas into simple, memorable symbols. He designed the logo for Hillary Clinton's 2016 presidential campaign.

Rob Janoff: The creator of the Apple logo with the rainbow-colored apple, which has become one of the most recognizable logos in the world. His work exemplifies the importance of creating logos that are both visually appealing and conceptually meaningful.

These designers have left an indelible mark on the field of graphic design through their iconic logos, innovative approaches, and enduring contributions to visual communication.

Notable typographers who have made significant contributions to the field of graphic design

Johannes Gutenberg: Although not a typographer in the modern sense, Gutenberg revolutionized the production of printed materials and laid the foundation for typography as we know it today with his invention of the movable type printing press in the 15th century.

Jan Tschichold: A German typographer, designer, and writer, Tschichold played a key role in the development of modern typography by advocating for the New Typography movement.

Eric Gill: An influential British typographer and sculptor, Gill is known for his typefaces such as Gill Sans and Perpetua, which have had a lasting impact on graphic design.

Claude Garamond: A French punch-cutter and type designer from the 16th century, Garamond created several enduring typefaces that are still widely used today, including Garamond and Sabon.

William Caslon: An English typefounder from the 18th century, Caslon is renowned for his Caslon typeface, which became one of the most popular and influential typefaces in English printing during the 18th and 19th centuries.

Adrian Frutiger: A Swiss typeface designer, Frutiger is best known for creating typefaces such as Univers, Frutiger, and Avenir. His work is characterized by its clarity, legibility, and versatility.

Hermann Zapf: A German typeface designer, Zapf created numerous typefaces, including Palatino, Optima, and Zapfino. His designs are known for their elegance, readability, and craftsmanship.

Paul Renner: A German type designer and typographer, Renner is best known for creating the typeface Futura, which has become a classic example of modernist typography and a staple of graphic design.

Matthew Carter: An English type designer, Carter has created many popular typefaces, including Georgia, Verdana, and Tahoma. His work spans both traditional and digital type design, and he has made significant contributions to the field of digital typography.

Josef Müller-Brockmann: A Swiss graphic designer and typographer, Müller-Brockmann was a leading figure in the Swiss Style movement. He is known for his minimalist and grid-based designs, which have had a profound influence on graphic design and typography.

Jonathan Hoefler and Tobias Frere-Jones: Founders of the Hoefler & Co. type foundry, Hoefler and Frere-Jones have created numerous acclaimed typefaces, including Hoefler Text, Gotham, and Mercury. Their work combines historical references with modern aesthetics and technical precision.

These are just a few examples of typographers who have made significant contributions to the field of graphic design. Their work continues to influence and inspire designers around the world.

Renowned illustrators across styles and genres

Some renowned illustrators who played important and versatile roles in varios areas of visual commmunication:

Quentin Blake: Is renowned for his collaboration with Roald Dahl. His whimsical and expressive illustrations have breathed life into many beloved children's books, such as Matilda and The BFG.

Maurice Sendak: An acclaimed American author and illustrator of children's books. He is most famous for his iconic work *Where the Wild Things Are,* Published in 1963, this book has since become one of the most beloved and celebrated children's books of all time.

Beatrix Potter: A renowned illustrator and author, Beatrix Potter is most celebrated for her delightful illustrations in beloved children's books such as *The Tale of Peter Rabbit.*

Dr. Seuss (Theodor Seuss Geisel): Widely recognized for his whimsical and imaginative illustrations, Dr. Seuss brought to life cherished characters and stories in iconic books like The *Cat in the Hat* and *Green Eggs and Ham.*

Norman Rockwell: Acclaimed for his nostalgic and heartwarming illustrations that graced the covers of *The Saturday Evening Post,* Norman Rockwell masterfully captured the essence of American life in the 20th century.

Hokusai: A Japanese ukiyo-e painter and printmaker, Hokusai achieved fame for his woodblock print series *Thirty-Six Views of Mount Fuji,* most notably *The Great Wave off Kanagawa.*

Edward Gorey: Renowned for his macabre and whimsical illustrations, Edward Gorey's distinctive style is evident in his work on books such as *The Gashlycrumb Tinies* and *The Doubtful Guest.*

Shaun Tan: An Australian illustrator and author, Shaun Tan's work, particularly in books like *The Arrival* and *The Lost Thing,* often delves into themes of immigration and identity through visually stunning and surreal illustrations.

Brian Froud: Celebrated for his fantasy illustrations, Brian Froud's work is closely associated with the world of Jim Henson's *The Dark Crystal* and *Labyrinth.*

Mary Blair: Known for her distinctive concept art and illustrations for Disney, Mary Blair made significant contributions to classics such as *Cinderella, Peter Pan,* and *Alice in Wonderland.*

Wendell Minor: A renowned American artist and illustrator, celebrated for his extensive body of work which includes over 2,000 book covers and numerous children's books. Throughout his career, Minor has collaborated with esteemed authors such as Jean Craighead George and Robert Burleigh. Some notable examples of his illustrations can be found in books such as *Reaching for the Moon* and *Galápagos George.*

Bill Mayer: An accomplished American illustrator, recognized for his exceptional talent in a variety of artistic fields. With a diverse portfolio, Mayer's work encompasses editorial illustrations, advertising projects, and book covers. He has had the privilege of contributing to major publications such as The New York Times, The Wall Street Journal, and TIME magazine. Mayer's illustrations are often characterized by a clever blend of wit, humor, and a profound understanding of storytelling.

Trevor Irvin: An American illustrator with an incredibly versatile portfolio, showcasing his expertise in a wide range of artistic styles. His work spans from traditional illustration to caricatures, and he is particularly notable for his skill in mascot and character creation. One of his most significant achievements was the creation of the Blaze mascot, originally intended for the 1996 Atlanta Olympics, which later became the iconic logo for the 1996 Atlanta Paralympics.

These illustrators have made a lasting impact on the world of visual storytelling, influencing generations of artists and captivating audiences with their unique styles and creativity. It's important to note that information on contemporary illustrators may not be as extensive as that of more established or historical figures. If you have specific questions or would like to explore their portfolios in more detail, we recommend visiting their official websites or contacting them directly if possible.

Helpful books for self-taught graphic designers

Here is a list of a few books that can help you with graphic design. They cover a range of topics, from design principles to specific software skills:

"The Non-Designer's Design Book" by Robin Williams

Description: This book is a great resource for beginners. It introduces fundamental design principles in a clear and accessible way. It covers topics like contrast, repetition, alignment, and proximity. It provides practical advice for creating visually appealing designs.

"Thinking with Type" by Ellen Lupton

Description: This book is a comprehensive guide to understanding and working with typography. It covers the history of typography, principles of letterforms, and practical tips for effective typography in design projects.

"Logo Design Love" by David Airey

Description: This book focuses on logo design. It provides insights into the process of creating memorable and effective logos. It covers design concepts, client communication, and showcases real world examples to inspire and educate.

"The Elements of User Experience" by Jesse James Garrett

Description: Understanding user experience (UX) is essential for graphic designers working on digital projects. This book breaks down the elements of UX design and provides a framework for creating user-centered and effective designs.

"Adobe Photoshop CC Classroom in a Book" by Andrew Faulkner and Conrad Chavez

Description: If you want to enhance your skills in Adobe Photoshop, this book is part of the official Adobe training series. It covers the essentials of Photoshop CC, offering step-by-step tutorials and hands-on projects to improve your proficiency in the software.

"Adobe InDesign, Illustrator & Photoshop - Graphic Design Portfolio" by Against The Clock

Description: This book offers a comprehensive understanding of the top three software applications used in graphic design: Photoshop, Illustrator, and InDesign. It includes detailed tutorials and practical projects that cover a variety of tasks commonly found in the field, preparing you for your career.

Remember to check for the latest editions or versions of these books, as the field of graphic design is dynamic and updates may have been released since this book was published. Additionally, consider exploring other resources based on your specific interests and needs within the vast and continually evolving field of graphic design.

Places where freelance graphic designers can discover job opportunities

Freelance graphic designers can discover job opportunities through various online platforms, networking, and self-promotion. Here are some places where freelance graphic designers can find job opportunities:

Upwork: This popular freelancing platform allows designers to create profiles and bid on projects across various design categories.

Fiverr: Freelancers can offer their services at different price points on this platform, attracting clients in need of specific design services.

Freelancer: Similar to Upwork, Freelancer is a competitive marketplace where freelancers can bid on projects, including graphic design gigs.

Toptal: Known for its rigorous screening process, Toptal connects freelancers with clients in search of top-tier professionals.

99designs: This platform focuses on design contests, where clients post briefs and designers submit their work to compete for projects.

Behance: Behance, a platform by Adobe, allows designers to showcase their portfolios and also features a "Job Board" section for design-related job opportunities.

Dribbble: Dribbble is a community where designers can showcase their work and attract clients for freelance projects.

SimplyHired: As a job search engine, SimplyHired aggregates freelance and remote job listings, making it easier for designers to find graphic design opportunities.

Remote OK: This job board specifically focuses on remote opportunities, connecting graphic designers with freelance and remote design jobs worldwide.

LinkedIn: Utilize LinkedIn to build a professional profile, connect with potential clients, and showcase your work. Join relevant groups and follow companies to stay updated on job opportunities and networking events.

To increase your chances of finding rewarding projects and building a successful freelance career, graphic designers should explore websites and publications related to their niche or target industries. By actively seeking out opportunities through these resources, you can maximize your potential for finding job listings or freelance opportunities.

Remember to tailor your profile or portfolio to each platform and actively engage with the community to increase your visibility. Building a strong online presence and consistently delivering quality work will contribute to a successful freelance career.

Is having a degree in graphic design necessary for success?

Obtaining a graphic design degree is not necessary for a career in the field. Many successful graphic designers have achieved success through self-learning, online courses, workshops, and practical experience. In the graphic design industry, skills, creativity, and a strong portfolio often carry more weight than formal education.

When deciding whether or not to pursue a degree in graphic design, consider the following factors:

Portfolio and Skills: Employers and clients prioritize a strong portfolio that showcases design skills and creativity. Regardless of educational background, a compelling portfolio is essential.

Self-Learning Opportunities: With the abundance of online resources, tutorials, and courses, individuals can teach themselves graphic design. This approach allows for flexibility and tailored learning.

Industry Recognition: Employers and clients in graphic design value the quality of work and ability to meet design needs. A well-curated portfolio and practical experience hold significant weight.

Networking and Experience: Building a network within the design community and gaining experience through internships, freelance work, or personal projects can be as valuable, if not more so, than formal education.

Cost and Time Considerations: Pursuing a degree can be costly and time-consuming. If these factors are important to you, exploring alternative paths like self-learning or shorter-term courses may be more practical.

Changing Industry Landscape: The design industry is evolving, with some employers placing greater emphasis on practical skills and experience rather than degrees.

Personal Goals: Consider your career goals and whether a degree aligns with them. Some design roles may require a degree, particularly in academic or specialized fields, while others prioritize skills and experience.

It's important to note that some individuals still choose to pursue a degree in graphic design for structured learning, mentorship opportunities, and access to educational resources.

Remember that ultimately, the decision to pursue a graphic design degree depends on your circumstances, goals, and preferences. If you choose not to pursue a degree, focus on building a strong portfolio, gaining practical experience, and staying updated on industry trends and technologies. Continual learning and a proactive approach to your career can lead to success in graphic design, with or without a formal degree.

Reputable universities known for their online graphic design programs

There are several reputable online universities that provide professional and recognized degrees in graphic design. However, it is important to verify the current accreditation status and program details directly from the universities' websites.

Savannah College of Art and Design (SCAD)
Programs: Bachelor of Fine Arts (BFA) and Master of Fine Arts (MFA) in Graphic Design
Website: SCAD Graphic Design Programs

Full Sail University
Program: Bachelor of Science (BS) in Graphic Design
Website: Full Sail Graphic Design Program

Academy of Art University
Programs: Bachelor of Fine Arts (BFA) and Master of Fine Arts (MFA) in Graphic Design
Website: Academy of Art Graphic Design Programs

Liberty University
Program: Bachelor of Fine Arts (BFA) in Graphic Design
Website: Liberty University Graphic Design Program

University of Florida (UF) Online
Program: Bachelor of Science (BS) in Digital Arts and Sciences with a specialization in Graphic Design
Website: UF Online Graphic Design Program

Maryland Institute College of Art (MICA)
Program: Master of Fine Arts (MFA) in Graphic Design
Website: MICA Graphic Design MFA

Sessions College for Professional Design
Program: Associate and Bachelor of Fine Arts (AFA/BFA) in Graphic Design
Website: Sessions College Graphic Design Programs

Penn State World Campus
Program: Bachelor of Design in Digital Multimedia Design
Website: Penn State World Campus Graphic Design Program

Rocky Mountain College of Art and Design (RMCAD)
Programs: Bachelor of Fine Arts (BFA) and Master of Fine Arts (MFA) in Graphic Design
Website: RMCAD Graphic Design Programs

Always verify the accreditation of the university and the specific graphic design program. Additionally, please note that program offerings and details may change, so it is advisable to contact the universities directly for the most up-to-date information.

DEFINITIONS OF SOME TERMS

Bleed:
In graphic design and printing, a bleed refers to the area of an image or design that extends beyond the final trim size of a printed piece.

Elements of design:
Color, line value, shape, form, texture

Hierarchy:
Hierarchy in typography refers to the visual arrangement of text elements to convey their relative importance.

Kerning:
Kerning refers to the adjustment of space between individual pairs of letters within a word or line of text.

Leading:
Leading (pronounced "ledding") pertains to the vertical space between lines of text.It determines the distance from the baseline of one line to the baseline of the next line.

Tracking:
Tracking involves adjusting the spacing uniformly across a range of characters within a block of text.

Legibility:
Legibility pertains to the design of the typeface and the shape of individual glyphs (characters). It focuses on the ability to distinguish one glyph from another when reading.

Principles of Design:
Emphasis, balance and alignment, repetition, proportion, movement, space.

Production Flat:
A production flat for a printed packaging box would include color swatches, graphics, and any special finishes (like embossing or foil stamping).

Readability:
Readability focuses on the overall reading experience and how easily we comprehend entire words, phrases, or blocks of text. While legibility deals with individual characters, readability encompasses the entire composition.

Sans Serif fonts:
The term "sans" means "without" in French. Sans serif fonts lack the decorative lines (serifs) found in serif fonts.

Serif Fonts:
Serif fonts have small lines or strokes (sometimes referred to as feet or tails) regularly attached to the end of larger strokes in letters or symbols within a particular font family.

Summary

The intent of this book is not to provide a step-by-step guide on becoming a graphic designer. Instead, it serves as a helpful resource and guide for understanding the core principles of graphic design. It emphasizes the importance of learning design programs and participating in graphic design communities. The book briefly touches on the significance of typography and color and offers a few beginner layout tips. Moreover, it addresses the importance of the design process in creating mockup solutions based on project briefs.

The book provides tips on creating compelling mockups and showcases creative mockup solutions created by university students who followed a simple design brief for each project. It includes inspiring images and encourages the use of online design templates for mockup creation from flyers to package design. The book also highlights the value of building a portfolio of mockups and provides advice on how to create an effective mockup portfolio. Additionally, it suggests exploring the design marketplace for further mockup inspiration.

In addition, the book discusses the significance of color in branding, and features AI-generated color wheels and touches on color palettes found in nature. The explanation of the RGB and CMYK color models is brief as is the type of color used for print and onscreen.

Other sections of the book explore finding a niche market and whether offering services for free at the start of a career is beneficial. It also addresses the question of whether having a website to showcase mockups is necessary, as well as the importance of obtaining a graphic design degree.

The book also offers a comprehensive list of resources recommended for self-taught designers. These resources cover various aspects such as books on the history of design, lists of renowned logo designers, notable typographers, and famous illustrators. The book also includes information on job opportunities and online universities that offer graphic design degrees.

The book concludes by presenting a design brief for a first mockup challenge and how to begin the journey, and provides information on where to find free project briefs to begin developing design mockups.

Graphic design is a valuable skill in various professions and not limited to the creative industry. Students pursuing careers in marketing, web development, or medicine can benefit from the ability to communicate visually. Graphic design education prepares students for a wide range of career paths. In today's job market, effective communication is highly sought after by employers. Even in non-design roles, professionals often need to create presentations, reports, and visuals to convey information clearly. Teaching design basics ensures that students are well-prepared for the demands of the modern workforce.

It is the author's hope that instructors of graphic design will find this book a useful resource and guide for their students in beginning graphic design courses.

About the Author—Maugé-Lewis

The author, an alumna of Howard University (Washington, DC), now a Professor Emerita at Kennesaw State University (KSU) in Georgia, has played a key role in developing and coordinating the Graphic Communication concentration in the School of Art and Design at KSU for over two decades. With her expertise and innovative approach, she has not only won awards for her design work but has also presented at numerous national and international conferences. In recognition of her contributions, she was selected as one of the twelve "Educators to Watch" by Graphic Design USA (GDUSA) in 2018. GDUSA, a renowned organization providing news and information to graphic designers and the broader creative community since 1963, continues to acknowledge her achievements. In 2021, she launched MaugeDesign, an award-winning online book cover design business. Additionally, in 2022, she received In-house Design awards, which led to her being invited as "A Person to Watch" by GDUSA. It is worth noting that Kennesaw State University has consistently been listed among GDUSA's Top Design Schools since 2015.

Maugé-Lewis has received the Distinguished Teaching Award in the College of the Arts at KSU twice. Under her guidance, her students have achieved remarkable success, winning awards at local, national, and international levels, including GDUSA, the Society of Publication Designers, and the "48 Hour Re-Pack" competitions among others. In 2009 her students secured both first and second places, as well as an honorable mention, in the first-ever Yellow Pages design competition, then won again in two successive competitions. The competition was short-lived and ended after three years.

Her main focus is maintainig excellence in teaching and ensuring student learning. Her teaching philosophy emphasizes learning the programs, building a strong foundation in graphic design fundamentals, problem-solving, and design-thinking. She strives to motivate and empower her students to succeed in a rapidly changing technological and diverse world and in finding fulfilling careers. Known for her direct and no-nonsense approach in the classroom, she sets high standards for her students. Some of her students now flourish as Art Directors, Brand Managers, Web Designers and Marketing specialists in the graphic design field – while some are carving out amazing careers at companies such as Disney, Facebook, and Apple, among others, with a few starting their own design businesses.

The author firmly believes that instructors face the challenges of effectively teaching graphic design fundamentals, problem-solving, and design-thinking skills that go beyond mere tutorials and projects. In addition to technical expertise, students also need to develop strong research, oral, and written communication skills. To address this, the author consistently assigned meaningful readings in her courses, which sparked class discussions in tandem with graphic design projects. These readings covered various topics, such as notable logo designers, typographers, color theorists, and modern design thinking theories. As future leaders, visual communicators, and advocates for local, national, and international issues, she contends that students must possess the necessary tools to tackle social problems, test their design thinking and creativity, and make a genuine impact. She also regularly contributes as a "Top Graphic Design Voice" on LinkedIn.

The purpose of this book is to share her philosophy and insights with three different groups: those who aspire to become graphic designers, design instructors in the field, and the broader design community. This is the first in a series of three books.

"

www.ingramcontent.com/pod-product-compliance
Lightning Source LLC
Chambersburg PA
CBHW041600110726
48005CB00002B/239

* 9 7 9 8 9 9 9 0 4 1 4 1 0 5 *